A Redemptorist Missionary in Ireland, 1851–1854
Memoirs by Joseph Prost, C.Ss.R.



IRISH NARRATIVES

IRISH NARRATIVES

Series edited by David Fitzpatrick

Personal narratives of past lives are essential for understanding any field of history. They provide unrivalled insight into the day-to-day consequences of political, social, economic or cultural relationships. Memoirs, diaries and personal letters, whether by public figures or obscure witnesses of historical events, will often captivate the general reader as well as engrossing the specialist. Yet the vast majority of such narratives are preserved only among the manuscripts or rarities in libraries and archives scattered over the globe. The aim of this series of brief yet scholarly editions is to make available a wide range of narratives concerning Ireland and the Irish over the last four centuries. All documents, or sets of documents, are edited and introduced by specialist scholars, who guide the reader through the world in which the text was created. The chosen texts are faithfully transcribed, the biographical and local background explored, and the documents set in historical context. This series will prove invaluable for university and school teachers, providing superb material for essays and textual analysis in class. Above all, it offers a novel opportunity for readers interested in Irish history to discover fresh and exciting sources of personal testimony.

Other titles in the series:

*Andrew Bryson's Ordeal: An Epilogue to the 1798 Rebellion*, edited by Michael Durey

*Henry Stratford Persse's Letters from Galway to America, 1821–1832*, edited by James L. Pethica and James C. Roy

*Frank Henderson's Easter Rising*, edited by Michael Hopkinson

Forthcoming titles:

*A Patriot Priest: A Life of Reverend James Coigly*, edited by Dáire Keogh

*'My Darling Danny': Letters from Mary O'Connell to her son Daniel, 1830–1832*, edited by Erin Bishop

David Fitzpatrick teaches history at Trinity College, Dublin. His books include *Politics and Irish Life, 1913–1921* (1977) and *Oceans of Consolation: Personal Accounts of Irish Migration to Australia* (1995).

# A Redemptorist Missionary in Ireland, 1851–1854

## Memoirs by Joseph Prost, C.Ss.R.

Translated and Edited by
Emmet Larkin and Herman Freudenberger

CORK UNIVERSITY PRESS

*For Diane and Paulette*

First published in 1998 by
Cork University Press
Cork
Ireland



Reprinted 2006



British Library Cataloguing in Publication Data

A CIP catalogue record for this book is available from the British Library.

ISBN 1 85918 160 0

Typesetting by Red Barn Publishing, Skeagh, Skibbereen
Printed by CPI Antony Rowe, Eastbourne

*Contents*

## *Acknowledgements*

It is a very great pleasure for us to be able to thank all those who have had a hand and part in the editing and translating of these memoirs. We must first of all, however, pay our respects to the memory of the late Father Alfred Schedl, who was the archivist of the Congregation of the Most Holy Redeemer in Vienna, for his great kindness and generosity in encouraging and expediting our work. We must also thank Fathers Walter H. George, Harry A. Grile and Gilbert A. Enderle, members of the Redemptorist community in Chicago, for their very significant contributions to the making of this volume. Father George generously secured for us a microfilm copy of the Prost memoirs, which greatly facilitated our work, and has been most helpful in encouraging this endeavour from its very inception. Father Grile read the whole of the manuscript, the translation, introduction and editorial notes, and made numerous valuable suggestions in regard to the correcting and improving of it. Father Enderle not only read the entire manuscript, but also brought his great learning and very considerable linguistic skills in German and Latin to bear in construing and translating some of the more difficult and recondite passages in the manuscript. Indeed, he has saved us from much grief and the reader from much pain, for which we cannot thank him enough.

We are also most grateful to Mr Ray Gadke, Microfilm Librarian of the Regenstein Memorial Library at the University of Chicago, for his help in securing a photocopy from the microfilm, and for reading the whole of the manuscript. We are also considerably obliged to Miss Michele O'Neill, our graduate assistant in the Department of History at the University of Chicago, who not only typed, copy-edited and proof-read the entire manuscript, but also helped prepare the index. Finally, we must thank the general editor of this series, Professor David Fitzpatrick of the Department of Modern History at Trinity College, Dublin, for his most careful attention to and suggestions for the improvement of this volume. We, of course, remain responsible for any of the errors that may yet be found in this volume.

## *Introduction*

Joseph Prost (1804–85), the author of this memoir of his experiences in Ireland from 1851 to 1854, was an Austrian Redemptorist priest who had an interesting and stormy life. He was born in Freinberg, Upper Austria, in the diocese of Linz, on 11 January 1804.[1] He received the greater part of his early education from a local priest, who, Prost later maintained, did not understand the meaning of piety.[2] He then studied philosophy at Linz, and in 1827 he joined the Premonstratensian Order in Schlägl and entered their novitiate. On completing his year's novitiate, the order sent him to the University of Vienna to pursue his academic studies. Prost quickly became disenchanted with the worldly life of the university, where he and his confrères were encouraged to read novels and poetry and to go to the theatre. 'We were actually', he later wrote, 'worldly gentlemen in priestly garb.'[3] He was soon attracted to the Redemptorists and their very able superior, Joseph Passerat, because of their great emphasis on holiness and piety. At Christmas 1829 Prost joined the Redemptorists formally and entered their novitiate. Because he had not taken his vows with the Premonstratensians, they released him from his obligations, and he received the Redemptorist habit on 23 January 1830. In the following year Prost took his vows as a Redemptorist at their house in Mautern in Styria on 24 March 1831, and some sixteen months later, on completing his course in theology, was ordained at Mautern on 29 July 1832.[4] He was then sent to the recently founded house in Leoben near Mautern, where for the next two and a half years he was engaged in parish work.

In late 1834 Father Passerat sent a circular letter to the members of the Austrian province asking for volunteers for the American mission.[5] Prost volunteered, and to his very great surprise he found himself, at the age of thirty-one and less than three years a priest, appointed by Passerat as superior of the Redemptorist mission in America. He arrived in New York in August 1835, and for the next six years he worked extremely hard to establish the Redemptorist community on a permanent basis in the United States.[6] In the face of some extraordinary difficulties and problems, not the least of which were his own inexperience and wilfulness, he succeeded in establishing Redemptorist houses in Rochester (New York), Pittsburgh and Baltimore. In early 1841 Prost was replaced as superior of the American mission by Alexander Czvitkovicz, the rector of the Redemptorist house in Vienna. After some very serious disagreements with the new superior, Prost was summarily dismissed by him from the Congregation.[7] In this awful crisis, Prost was rescued by his old friend, John Hughes, the Bishop of New York, who provided for him in a German-speaking parish in Utica, New York, where he ministered happily for more than a year, until he was finally able to return to Vienna in early 1843.[8] Because Czvitkovicz did not have the right to dismiss Prost from the Congregation, and had therefore acted uncanonically, Passerat and his consultors forgave all and welcomed him home. He was soon assigned to a parish mission group working in and around Innsbruck and in the Tyrol. Prost continued to conduct parish missions for some five years until May 1848, when the Congregation was suppressed in the Austrian dominions in the revolution of that year and he and his colleagues were driven into exile.

Many of the Austrian Redemptorists, including Prost, found refuge in the Belgian province of the Congregation, which then included Holland and England.[9] Because of the serious manpower shortage in England, Prost was assigned to the struggling English mission at the request of its superior, Frederick de Held. In spite of his having served some seven years in America, Prost's spoken English apparently still left a good deal to be desired because most of his missionary work in the United States had been done among German-Americans. Shortly after his arrival in England in 1848, Prost was assigned to the new Redemptorist foundation at Llanherne in Cornwall, where he was tutored in English by one of the local Carmelite nuns and rapidly acquired a considerable fluency and proficiency in the language.[10] After serving during the next few years as superior of a number of the smaller English houses, all of which were eventually closed in an effort to concentrate manpower and resources and to increase the efficiency of the Congregation's parish mission work, Prost was appointed superior of the new Redemptorist foundation at Bishop Eton, near Liverpool, in June 1851.[11] At the same time he was also appointed superior and director of parish missions in England, with a view to extending them to Ireland as well.

Soon after the founding of the new house at Bishop Eton the English superior, Frederick de Held, had conversations in Ireland in September 1851 with William Monsell, the influential Catholic convert and member of parliament for County Limerick, about establishing a foundation in Ireland in order to further the work of parish missions in that country.[12] Monsell apparently introduced de Held to the Bishop of Limerick, John Ryan, who invited him to give a mission in his cathedral parish of St John's in Limerick city. In October 1851, therefore, Prost and four confrères arrived in Limerick and conducted a very successful two-week mission, after which the missioners were the house guests of Monsell at his country estate at Tervoe, near Limerick. Monsell raised the question of the Redemptorists establishing a house in the diocese, and Prost was encouraged by the idea. During the next several months, while Prost was absent giving missions in England and then on holiday in Germany, his colleagues continued to conduct missions and to preach charity sermons in Ireland.[13] In the meantime the Bishop of Limerick requested another mission from de Held for his second mensal parish of St Michael's in Limerick city and Prost was quickly recalled from his holiday to direct the mission. The mission, which lasted for some three weeks, from 16 May to 7 June 1852, was, like the first, enormously successful. During the mission the missioners resided at a house in Bank Place rented for them by Monsell, which in the following year formally became their first foundation in Ireland.

After the second Limerick mission in June 1852 Prost began to spend more and more time in Ireland arranging and conducting parish missions and he soon evolved a mission mode and style that proved to be both unique and original. Prost early became aware that there were a number of serious abuses connected with giving parish missions in Ireland. Most of these abuses had mainly to do with the problem of how to provide for the expenses of the mission. In order to provide for the travel, room and board and a reasonable honorarium for the missioners, the local parish priest usually had to charge admission and make collections during the mission. Some of the parish priests were also anxious to realise a profit from the mission, over and above what was necessary to provide for the missioners, because they had mortgages and debts outstanding on their churches and schools. Because of the expenses incurred, moreover, the mission often had to be terminated before the confessions of all the penitents were heard, and many sinners, therefore, remained in their original and dreadful state of spiritual destitution. Prost undertook to remedy the situation by a comprehensive reform of the system of financing parish missions. The culmination of his efforts may be seen in the requirements he insisted on in arranging for a mission in the parish of Wexford with the parish priest of that town, James Roche, just one year after the second mission in Limerick city.

'As I myself', Prost explained to Roche on 30 May 1853, 'shall come to Wexford soon, I think it is best we settle all when I am there. But now I must make some remarks. Your parish is very numerous and your church does not hold the half part of your parish. It will therefore be necessary to preach outside, i.e. in the beautiful square joined to the church and convent. But if we must preach outside, we must choose a good season when we can expect good weather.'[14] 'We can accept no mission', he informed Roche, 'except under the following conditions:

(1) The entrance into the chapel during the whole time of the mission must be *entirely free* and no collectors are allowed to stand at the *door* of the church, or at the *gate* of the churchyard.
(2) *No collection* is allowed during the mission *for other purposes.*
(3) His Lordship the Bishop must sanction the mission, and grant to the missionaries all faculties, ordinary and extraordinary. His Lordship must also be so kind as to give leave for Expositions of

the Blessed Sacrament and benedictions, as we are accustomed to do in our mission, and for the erection of a mission cross in a suitable place as a memorial of the mission to which general indulgences will be attached granted by his present Holiness.

(4) The superior of the mission must have full liberty to direct and to arrange all, because two superiors would cause only confusion.

(5) The missionaries must have full liberty in prolonging the mission and to take as much time for it as they think proper in order to do their work well. Hence no time can be appointed for the end of the mission. And as the missionaries have to give so many missions, they will not stay one day longer than is necessary.

(6) *The missionaries ask nothing else except the use of the church, and a house and poor furniture. For all the rest, i.e. kitchen etc. etc., they themselves provide of their own expense.*

(7) No public collection for the expenses of the missionaries is allowed. If there should be some who wish to contribute to their expenses, they can do so privately, *but nobody is to be asked*, and all is left entirely to their free will without the least *compulsion* or *begging*. We know very well the wants of the Catholic churches in Ireland and we would be very glad if we could procure money for them, but our Rule teaches us and we know it by our own experience *that the least money speculation at a mission destroys all the fruits of a mission, and if one penny, or even only a half-penny would be asked at the door, many sinners would remain away and be lost, for whose conversion the missionaries come*. There are also good families *for whom a mission* is most beneficial. Their appearance is *very often very respectable*, but they are poor, and if only a penny would be asked *from them they would be obliged to remain away*. In order to derive fruits from a mission, it is not enough to hear some sermons, they must follow the whole course of all sermons and instructions as much as possible; *but if only a half-penny would be asked or a penny* and if there be 4 or 5 persons in a family, their daily expense for hearing a sermon etc. would deprive them of their necessary meals, and consequently they would be obliged *to*

> *remain away.* We know the *necessity of collections*, but for the reasons mentioned above missions must make an exception from the general rule. And lest we may yield to the entreaties on such occasions, higher superiors *command us to stop the mission as soon as one would begin to place collectors at the door etc. and to leave the place.*

'I mention this', Prost advised Roche, 'lest one may accuse us of unkindness or of want of regard to the wants of the church etc. and that each one may see that we are bound in conscience to act in this manner.'

'Although all have free access to all our sermons and instructions etc., [both] parishioners and strangers,' Prost further observed, 'to the confessionals, however, only those belonging to the parish are admitted, with the exclusion of all the strangers without exception. This is necessary to secure for the parishioners the benefit of confession during the mission. Without this regulation the mission would be changed into a pilgrimage. This would ruin the fruits of the mission.' 'The principal thing in a mission', he maintained, 'is to hear the sermons and instructions which prepare and dispose for confession. This is why confessions in a mission are better.' 'If they', Prost added, referring to sinners, 'would come only to confession without hearing the sermons, drawn by the novelty, or by the desire to escape their own pastor, etc., etc., I do not know what to say of such confessions, and the impudence of such intruding strangers would prevent the parishioners from confession, which is so necessary for them in order to settle their consciences, which is [*sic*] excited by listening to the sermons.' 'As your parish is so large,' Prost again pointed out, 'we must request the assistance of all the Reverend Fathers of Wexford in hearing confessions.' 'As your parish is large,' he then finally reminded Roche, '*we will come in a large number, but do not be puzzled by it, because we find easily room in a small house. The beds must be very simple as the fathers do not like to sleep in feather beds, we like open beds the best. And as our journey and boarding is all at our own expense, nobody is burdened if we come in considerable number.*'

This Wexford mission, in which seven Redemptorists laboured for six weeks, from 14 August to 25 September 1853, was Prost's crowning achievement in Ireland. After Wexford, though he continued to serve on missions for more than a year, his influence and authority were clearly on the decline. The reasons for Prost's eclipse were a combination of the personal and the political. His colleagues apparently were not all happy with his views regarding the reform of the missions and his subordinates found him a hard task master and did not always take kindly to his interpretation of the rules. He was, moreover, a political outsider in the Belgian province. His colleagues in England and Ireland were virtually all Belgian or Belgian-trained Dutchmen and Englishmen, and by 1853 there had developed some very serious differences of opinion between the members of the Belgian and German provinces about how the Transalpine Congregation should be governed. Prost was considered to be a German partisan and a supporter of the current Vicar General of the Transalpine Congregation, Rudolph von Smetana. In 1853 both sides were obviously manoeuvering for political advantage in regard to the expected General Chapter, at which a new Rector Major of the whole Congregation would be elected. Prost, it appears, was a casualty in the ensuing struggle for power between the Belgians and the Germans.

In March 1854 he was replaced as superior of the parish missions in England and Ireland by Bernard Hafkenscheid, a Dutchman, who had just returned from America, where he had been superior and then provincial for the previous four years. Hafkenscheid was also appointed superior of the new foundation recently made in Limerick. At Hafkenscheid's request, Prost continued to serve on those missions he had arranged before Hafkenscheid's arrival in order to preserve continuity, but he soon became deeply disturbed by the radical changes made by the new superior in the procedures and mode of conducting missions in Ireland. Hafkenscheid was determined to make the missions profitable because he planned to build a new church and residence in Limerick for which he badly needed funds. Prost was also distressed by what he viewed as Hafkenscheid's emotionalism and sensationalism in preaching at the missions. Hafkenscheid had acquired a formidable reputation as a preacher in both Europe and America, and by all accounts his presence in the pulpit was extraordinary. Inevitably, Prost and Hafkenscheid quarrelled and when Prost was then replaced as superior of Bishop Eton in late 1854, he realised that his usefulness in England and Ireland was at an end, and he decided to request his return to the Austrian province.

On his return to Vienna in 1855, Prost received a very frosty reception from his Austrian brethren, who apparently felt that he had not pulled his weight as a German in the recent struggle for power in the Congregation. He was then assigned to his old college at Mautern where he had done his theology and had been ordained. At Mautern, while engaged in pastoral work, Prost began to write a history of the founding of the American mission from 1832 to 1843, in which he had played so large a part. He completed his manuscript in January 1857, and, as he explained in his foreword, the 'following history is not written to be published, but for our archives as a source to draw on when a history of our Congregation will be written'.[15] Later that summer Prost was ordered by the Austrian provincial to Puchheim in Lower Austria. That community apparently was not very happy about having to receive him, and shortly afterwards, in late September 1857, the provincial sent him to the new novitiate at Katzelsdorf in Lower Austria, where he was also not very welcome.[16] On 10 January 1858 the provincial arrived unexpectedly in Katzelsdorf and informed Prost that the Rector Major in Rome, Nicholas Mauron, had appointed him superior of the Redemptorist mission to the Danish Virgin Islands and had ordered him to leave immediately.[17]

Prost left for Vienna the next day, 11 January 1858, his fifty-fourth birthday and sailed from Southampton for the West Indies on 2 February. He landed in St Thomas on 1 March, and three days later he arrived in Christiansted in St Croix and took possession as pastor of the parish of the Holy Cross, where he was to serve for the next two and a half years.[18] Some eleven weeks later, on 19 May, he was joined by Father Louis Dold and Brother Henry Voss. The Bishop of Roseau, Michael

Vesque, however, whose diocese included the islands of St Thomas and St Croix, insisted that Dold be sent as pastor to St Thomas, because the parish of SS Peter and Paul was not only without a resident priest but in a state of schism. Prost complied, but immediately wrote to his superiors explaining the situation and requesting more help. Eventually two more priests were sent, but Dold, who had become very ill, was obliged to return to Europe. A decision now had to be made about whether the small Redemptorist community of three priests and a brother should be divided between the two islands, or be concentrated in one or the other. The decision was eventually made in favour of St Thomas, and Prost was ordered home and left St Croix on 7 October 1860.[19] While in St Croix, Prost had become involved as superior in a quarrel with the Danish governor of the islands, who required that the Redemptorists take an oath of allegiance to the government.[20] Prost wrote to the authorities in Rome requesting permission to publish his correspondence with the governor. The Rector Major refused permission, but Prost apparently published a part of the correspondence before he left St Croix. For his insubordination, Prost was prohibited on his return home from participating in missions for six years.[21]

On his arrival home in early 1861, he was assigned to the Redemptorist community in Bornhofen, about ten miles south of Koblenz in Germany. In 1862 Prost was sent once again to Puchheim, of which he had unhappy memories from the months before being sent to the West Indies. To keep busy, he began to write a chronicle of the house, but he was soon replaced in that endeavour. He then wrote a memorandum on the reform of the parish mission system in 1865 for the consideration of a future General Chapter of the Congregation, which he submitted to the provincial, who never returned it to him.[22] The memorandum obviously owed a great deal to Prost's experience in Ireland in the 1850s. The main proposals included: the formal establishment of a second novitiate where priests would be properly trained for the parish missions; that the missions should be of longer duration; that the costs of the mission should be born entirely by the Congregation; that the children's missions should be an integral part of the parish missions;

and that there should be a closer collaboration with the Catholic press in promoting the parish missions.[23] Prost also wrote about this time on a number of other controversial subjects, such as the 'Equality of Confessions', and a 'Free Church in Free State', which was based on his American experience. He submitted these to his provincial for censorship, but he never heard any more about them. Finally, in 1869, he published the memorandum he had completed in 1865 on the reform of the parish missions as a brochure. It caused an uproar in the Congregation. He was required to do three days' public penance by the local bishop as his punishment for his inordinate pride.[24]

Prost, however, doggedly persevered with his writing, and by 1876 he had apparently completed his memoirs in two parts. The first was entitled 'My Experiences from the Time of My Return from America in 1843 to the Present 1874', and the second 'My Experiences in England, Ireland and the West Indies'.[25] The first manuscript consisted of 883 pages, and the second of 266. The first was essentially a chronological narrative, while the second was apparently meant to supplement the first and was more thematic and theoretical than historical in its content. By the time he completed these manuscripts in 1876 Prost was nearly blind, and the last sections of the 1843–74 narrative are in another hand and obviously were dictated. Prost was also by this time a very lonely and isolated figure, and his final comments in his memoirs are indeed as touching as they are sad. 'When one is decent to other people,' Prost observed, 'one has a right to expect kindness and friendship in return.'[26] 'When, however,' he added, 'one sits alone, half-blind for years and years without anyone talking to him, then this is certainly no small sorrow.' 'When I was still able to read and write,' he explained, 'I was able to take all this with greater ease. But since I have become nearly blind, this cross is extremely hard to bear. I have had as a result even thoughts of suicide.' 'God only knows', he finally confessed, 'what would have happened if I had not prayed.' Prost had to endure his private purgatory for yet another nine years. He was finally liberated when he died at Puchheim on 19 March 1885, at the age of eighty-one.[27]

The general significance and meaning of Prost's life, of course, remains a question for his future biographer, but even in this cursory survey of his career, it is quite evident that the parish mission movement was a central concern in his life after his return from America in 1843. His three-year career in Ireland, moreover, was crucial to his own development as a parish missioner because it was in Ireland that his ideas about parish missions as a system finally crystallised. The model he worked out in Ireland, and eventually articulated in the brochure he published in 1869, was never really fully implemented either in Ireland or elsewhere by the Redemptorists, but his practical work in founding the Congregation in Ireland, and inaugurating their parish mission movement there was to prove of enormous significance and importance for the religious practices of the Irish people in the aftermath of the Great Famine.

Indeed, the parish mission movement was the single most important factor in the making and consolidating of the Devotional Revolution that took place in Ireland between 1850 and 1880.[28] Within the space of a single generation the majority of the Irish people were transformed into those pious and practising Catholics they have essentially remained almost to the present day. The first formal parish mission in Ireland was given by the Irish Vincentian fathers in the town of Athy in the diocese of Dublin in November and December 1842. The Rosminians began their parish missions in Ireland in 1848, and the Jesuits in 1850. They were followed by the Redemptorists in 1851, the Passionists in 1855, and the Oblates in 1856. Soon afterwards the older religious orders in Ireland, such as the Dominicans, Franciscans, Capuchins and Augustinians, all also began to give parish missions. In the twenty-five years after the first Vincentian mission in 1842, therefore, not only were virtually all of the thousand parishes in Ireland visited by the missioners of the above religious orders, but by 1880 nearly all of those parishes had been visited again, and some even a third and a fourth time.[29] The cumulative effect of these more than 2,000 missions was a remarkable national religious revival that profoundly affected both the character of the Irish Catholic people and the course of their history.

The Redemptorist contribution to this Devotional Revolution was very impressive. Of the approximately 2,000 missions given in Ireland between 1842 and 1880, the Redemptorists accounted for some 350 in the thirty years between 1851 and 1880.[30] In addition, they conducted a large number of spiritual exercises in those years which included more than 160 retreats to priests and nuns, as well as some 450 retreats to the laity, not to mention the numerous sermons, novenas and *tridua*. By 1879, moreover, they had established sixty-two branches of the Confraternity of the Holy Family for men and women, totalling 62,000 members, of which the Limerick branch alone contained more than 3,000 members.[31] By 1900 the Redemptorists had become the premier missionary order in Ireland. In the twenty years between 1881 and 1900, for example, they averaged 35 missions and 77 spiritual exercises a year, and in 1900 they conducted 74 missions and 111 spiritual exercises for the clergy and laity.[32] Over the next decade, 1901-10, they averaged an extraordinary 95 missions and 205 spiritual exercises a year.[33] In the sixty years since their foundation in 1851, therefore, the Redemptorists had increased their apostolic labours in Ireland by more than 800 per cent — a quantitative achievement that certainly speaks for itself.

The achievement, however, had not only a quantitative dimension but a qualitative one as well. The purpose of preaching the instructions and the sermons during the course of the day was to heighten, in a cumulative way, the penitent's consciousness of sin and bring him to a realisation of the catastrophic consequences for his immortal soul if he should die in a state of sin. On each succeeding day of the mission the penitent was made more acutely aware of all the various ways in which he might have forsaken God, and reminded that if he did not confess his sincere repentance for his transgressions, he would lose the reward of heaven and win the torments of hell for all eternity. Since no one could be sure when his end would come and death usurp all good intentions, the time for reconciliation with God was at that moment. The multitudes that flocked to the confessionals at the mission were a true witness to the effectiveness of the Redemptorist preaching. The most remarkable moment of the mission, however, was its closing. During the last day a large stone mission cross, with a suitable inscription and date, was raised with great solemnity in the church and chapel yard to commemorate the mission and to serve as a visible reminder to the faithful both of their recent triumph over sin and death and of their solemn promise to persevere in their new-found state of grace. In the evening, after the closing sermon, the people assembled in their thousands in and around the church or chapel, each with a lighted taper, and renewed their baptismal vows by renouncing sin, evil and Satan.[34]

This extraordinary religious revival, however, not only transformed the religious practices of the majority of the Irish people; it also provided them with a new national cultural identity. Indeed, after the Famine there emerged a new and distinctive mindset — Irish Catholicism, which was characterised by a moral rigorism, a pious intensity and a sexual puritanism that profoundly affected popular values and mores. In this new mindset, or *mentalité*, Irish and Catholic became one and the new national cultural identity was forged. By becoming more intensely and militantly Catholic, the people were assured that they would never be absorbed or assimilated by the greater English culture as their Scottish and Welsh brethren had been because the historical identity of that English culture was itself profoundly rooted in its Protestantism and could not, therefore, without becoming something other than it was, accommodate the new Ultramontane and Tridentine Catholicism that had emerged in Ireland with the making and consolidating of the Devotional Revolution after the Famine.

## *Editorial Note*

Wherever we considered that it would be helpful or of interest to record the original German form of any word in Prost's text, we have included it (in italics within round parentheses) after the translated word. All Latin expressions appearing in the text are accompanied by English translations in square brackets. Occasional obscurities are clarified within square brackets. All instances of direct speech have been placed within inverted commas (never used by Prost) for the sake of intelligibility. Major gaps in the notebook text, involving the omission of material not concerning Ireland, are noted at the relevant points in the text. Insignificant minor elisions are denoted by the device of three points within square brackets.

Redemptorist Parish Missions in Ireland, 1851–1854

## *The Redemptorist Mission in Ireland, 1851–54: Itinerary*

(See map for the location, incidence and date of the missions)

| *Type of work* | *Date* | *Place* | *Diocese* |
|---|---|---|---|
| **1851** | | | |
| *Retreat: nuns | 13–21 Sept. | Loreto Sisters, Omagh | Derry |
| *Sermon | 14 Sept. | Omagh | Derry |
| *Sermon | 21 Sept. | Cappagh | Derry |
| Mission and children's mission | 19 Oct.–2 Nov. | St John's, Limerick | Limerick |
| *Mission | 9–23 Nov. | Omagh | Derry |
| **1852** | | | |
| *Sermon | 18 Jan. | St Michael's, Dublin | Dublin |
| *Mission | 16 Apr.–9 May | Derry | Derry |
| *Sermon | 18 Apr. | Cork churches | Cork |
| Mission | 16 May–7 June | St Michael's, Limerick | Limerick |
| Retreat: clergy | 20–23 June | Dublin | Dublin |
| *Mission | 20 June–7 July | St Andrew's, Dublin | Dublin |
| *Retreat: nuns | 15–18 Aug. | Sisters of Mercy, Dublin | Dublin |
| Mission | 12 Sept.–3 Oct. | Enniskillen | Clogher |
| Mission | 10 Oct.–1 Nov. | Waterside | Derry |
| Holiday | 6–17 Nov. | St Columb's, Derry | Derry |
| Mission | 21 Nov.–14 Dec. | Letterkenny | Raphoe |
| **1853** | | | |
| Mission | 3–31 Jan. | Omagh | Derry |
| Mission | 8 May–6 June | Gorey | Ferns |
| Mission | 8 May–6 June | Workhouse, Gorey | Ferns |
| House hiring | June | Bank Place, Limerick | Limerick |
| *Mission | 19 June–17 July | Randalstown | Down and Connor |
| Retreat: clergy | 4–9 July | St Peter's College, Wexford | Ferns |
| Retreat: boarders | 30 July–Aug. | Laurel Hill Convent, Limerick | Limerick |
| Retreat: nuns | 8–15 Aug. | Sisters of Mercy, Wexford | Ferns |
| Mission | 14 Aug.–25 Sept. | Franciscan Church, Wexford | Ferns |

| *Type of work* | *Date* | *Place* | *Diocese* |
|---|---|---|---|
| *Children's missions (2) | 25 Sept.–17 Oct. | Letterkenny | Raphoe |
| | | Omagh | Derry |
| Mission | 17 Oct.–13 Nov. | Strabane | Derry |
| Children's mission | Dec. | St Michael's, Limerick | Limerick |
| **1854** | | | |
| Mission | Mar. | New Ross (with Hafkenscheid) | Ferns |
| Retreat: lay | Apr. | Workhouse, New Ross | Ferns |
| Mission | 8 May | North Parish, Cork | Cork |
| *Mission | 24 June | Mallow | Cloyne |
| *Mission | 5–28 July | Barntown | Ferns |
| *Mission | 5–28 July | Glynn | Ferns |
| *Mission | July | St Alphonsus', Limerick | Limerick |
| Retreat: clergy | July | Wexford | Ferns |
| *Retreat: lay | July | Workhouse, Wexford | Ferns |
| Retreat: clergy | Aug. | St Jarlath's, Tuam | Tuam |
| Sermons (2) | Aug. | St Jarlath's, Tuam | Tuam |
| Conferences: nuns (2) | Aug. | Sisters of Mercy, Tuam | Tuam |
| | | Ursuline Sisters, Tuam | Tuam |
| *Mission | 29 Sept. | Athenry | Tuam |
| Mission | 7–31 Oct. | St Finbarr's, Cork | Cork |
| *Children's mission | 7 Oct. | St Finbarr's, Cork | Cork |
| Sermons: nuns (2) | 7 Oct. | Sisters of Mercy, Cork | Cork |
| | | Ursuline Sisters, Cork | Cork |
| Sermon | 1–7 Nov. | St Alphonsus', Limerick | Limerick |

* Prost absent.

# *Joseph Prost, C.Ss.R.*

Narrative of the Redemptorist Mission in Ireland, 1851–1854

*Extracted from*
'My Experiences from the Time of my Return from America in 1843 to the Present 1874'

[Prost Notebooks I–III:
Archives of the Austrian Redemptorist Province, Vienna]

[Notebook I, p. 1]

*Preface*

I have previously written up my experiences in America, and they are located in the archives of the provincial in Baltimore.

Now I want to write down my experiences honestly since my return so that they can be used by my successors for their instruction. I will attempt to connect my observations, experiences and judgements with each other. While reading this one will quickly find that I am not writing for my own glorification. Because I am writing for the instruction of others, I will point especially to errors and faults (*Gebrechen*). This will not be to the liking of everyone *nam veritas in multis odium parit* [for truth gives rise to hatred in many people]. One prefers to read praise, but that tends to induce false pride and will be of little use. Medicine is bitter, but it restores one's health. And thus to our work in God's name.

One of the Fathers who is highly respected in the Congregation and has served it well urged me to do this. I did not wish to do this, because I would be forced to say things that were uncomfortable and would be damaging. He told me, however, that it would be *pro bono comuni* [for the common good]. Thereupon I relented and decided to undertake the chore. I wish to note, however, that this is not written for publication. I will turn these writings over to the Father who urged me to this task and allow him to dispose of this as his conscience will guide him, either to use at some chapter meeting or elsewhere *ad bonum Congregationis* [for the good of the Congregation]. I am too old and for various reasons totally deprived of all influence, so that every word that I speak and every syllable that I write could be more damaging than useful. Someone else may derive some benefit from this. The reader will note, however, that I speak only the truth and without any partisanship. One will also see that I hold strictly to the principles of St Alphonsus.[1] Some may say that my writings leave something to be desired; I will readily agree to that. But I will nevertheless hold rigorously to the principles of St Alphonsus. I will add to this what may seem strange: I was too obedient and had too much candour (*Aufrichtigkeit*). If I were more deficient in these virtues, I would be in better shape.

[*The remaining pages of Notebook I (pp. 2–178) deal with the period from Prost's return to Austria from America in 1843 to his arrival in England in 1848.*]

[Notebook II, pp. 105–197]

Note: For the use and instruction of those who come after me, also to make us humble, which is the beginning of all holiness. Talk of glorification makes people proud and blind, therefore in these writings our errors and our faults are emphasised.

[*The first part of Notebook II (pp. 1–104) treats mainly of Prost's missionary work in England from 1849 to 1852.*]

## *I. Historical Background*

*Thus it went until 1829, the year in which the great O'Connell was able to prevail in parliament and to provide for the Emancipation of the Catholics.* For this Emancipation, however, the Catholics had to make two sacrifices, namely, the legal existence of the religious orders and the requirement that Catholic priests and monks could not appear in public in clerical dress. The punishment for such an infraction was £50. Before Emancipation the Catholics were not allowed to have public services anywhere in the Empire. The only exceptions were the Catholic chapels in the foreign embassies in London. In Ireland, in Dublin the Catholics used private residences as churches. They broke through the floors on every level and built galleries so that the parishioners could view the altar below. But when large numbers gathered for a service on one occasion the galleries collapsed and hundreds lost their lives and hundreds were injured. This occurrence caused even the Protestants to be stricken with sorrow and compassion. Many [Protestants] began to remark that Catholics were not allowed to have a public church. As a result, the Catholics were gradually allowed to build churches. Thus advances were made and, as a matter of fact, quite rapidly, all as a result of the willingness of the poor Catholic people to sacrifice financially without any help from the government. The people also had to find the resources for the support of the bishops and priests. But as Bishop Milner[2] said: With the end of the persecutions our enthusiasm slackened. The Irish Catholics at present rely much too much on the good works of their forebears.

Their forebears had to travel for hours to hear a Holy Mass and to receive the Holy Sacraments. During my stay in England and Ireland I was able to bring many Irish people, who lived close to the church and who had become too lazy to go there, to participate in the church services. As an example a priest in Liverpool showed me an entire street in which the Irish lived and who were too lazy to go to church. And at the same time they believe and maintain that they are the best Catholics in the world. With them being Irish and Catholic are identical as is English and Protestant. Their bishops and priests are no longer what they were during the time of persecution. The bishops are 'lords' and live like them, and the priests are true 'gentlemen', and they take their ease when it comes to attending to souls. Usually they heard confessions only during the day. In the evening they took their meals with the rich and prominent Catholics. Consequently the working people could not go to confession. While the living quarters of the priests were those of 'gentlemen', the churches were very miserable. To be sure, there were exceptions, but this was the rule. The priests were often French rigorists. The persecutions had caused many in Ireland to go to Heaven as martyrs, but after they ceased many bad habits remained.

The discipline and order of the religious communities had become seriously lax, with the exception of the Jesuits, Vincentians and the teaching brothers, as well as several female orders; but all these were new establishments after the persecution and had been brought in from the outside. I found among the clergy little enthusiasm for prayer or devotion. I found clergymen who kept the Eucharist in a box in their room and who carried it around in their pockets so that they could immediately administer it to sick people. During the time of persecution this was necessary, but it was also adhered to thereafter. I saw priests being rough and rude with the poor, but with the rich and prominent they were very courteous and polite; bishops and priests were dependent on the offerings of the faithful; they had nothing else, but they were very sharp in their demands for offerings.

The nationalistic spirit of the German clergy has also taken root among the Irish. In their fear of offending the Protestants, they made use of clever subterfuges that are also found in our [German] countries, i.e. in respect to religious exercises. It was different in their sermons, which were often deliberately controversial (*Controversiae*). The Catholics liked it when the Protestants were abused chapter and verse (*verkapitelt*) from the altars. And as with us formerly, the *Dogmata* [dogmas] were ignored in the sermons and only moralising and emotional matters were included; thus the Irish clergy eschew morals and the devotional and concentrate on the *Controverse* [*sic*]. The clergy were masterful in politics. And that is a great good fortune for Ireland, otherwise the Catholics would not have been able to achieve Emancipation or to make use of the rights that they have acquired.

Despite all these failings of the clergy, the people continued to hold them in exceptionally high regard. I saw how common people allowed themselves to be abused and to be struck without grumbling. They still look upon their bishop and priest as their persecuted fathers and reward them liberally (*reichlich*). The people are enthusiastic about their rights and the independence of their church. After Emancipation the English government made offers to pay the salaries of the bishops and clergy in Ireland on the condition that it would retain a veto [over the appointment of bishops]. Some of the bishops and clergy were willing to take this *Danâe* [Greek] gift, but the people said: 'No! We want the Catholic Church to be independent.'

I have already related that the old orders in Ireland, such as the Franciscans, the Capuchins and the Dominicans, had very seriously declined. It was different with the newly introduced orders such as the Jesuits, the missioners of St Vincent de Paul, or Lazarists, the teaching brothers and the nuns, etc. etc. One of the first religious communities that was introduced after the Catholics had a little room for manoeuvre was the Ursulines in Cork, where they now have a magnificent teaching institution. They were followed by the 'Presentation Nuns', i.e. Nuns of the Marian Sacrifice. In addition there are the Sisters of Loretto. These are our English ladies (*Fräuleins*) who originally came from Bavaria to England and then to Ireland and named their convent and church Loretto. Consequently their name was 'Loretto Nuns'.

In 1830 a new female religious order was created in Dublin in the following way: A pious Catholic girl[3] was adopted by a childless Protestant couple. This young lady was treated so well by her adoptive parents that she was eventually able to bring both into the Catholic Church and to a holy (*seliges*) end. During the lifetime of her adoptive parents this young lady expressed great sympathy for the female servants (*Dienstboten*) who when they lost their position often fell into dissolute (*liederlich*) ways. Therefore she always kept a large room available for such unemployed persons. After her adoptive parents died she inherited their property and thus was able greatly to extend her work of mercy (*Barmherzigkeit*). Other pious girls and women then joined in this effort. This community took these unemployed girls into their house, where they had to work in order to contribute towards their upkeep. They instructed these girls in work, religion and piety, and thereby restored them again to a normal life. As these ladies formed a community for the purpose of these acts of benevolence, they had to formulate rules for their community. At this point they came to the realisation that they must create a religious association. The Jesuits of Dublin drew up the rules for them and Archbishop Murray of Dublin[4] approved them. The first members of this community made a kind of novitiate in another convent in order to learn about convent life. They in turn instructed the others, and then they all took simple vows. In the end they finally received the approval of the Pope. They are called the 'Sisters of Mercy'. Those sisters associated with St Vincent de Paul are called the 'Sisters of Charity,' i.e. *sorores charitatis*, sisters of neighbourly love. The mother house of the 'Sisters of Mercy' is in Barclay [Baggot] Street, Dublin. It is an imposing (*grossartig*) institution. I at one time gave a retreat there. Their chapel is a beautiful little church that is filled with nuns and their girls seeking asylum (*unflucht*). I offered a Solemn High Mass in it once with the organ and a fine choir.

The convent personnel consists of choir sisters and lay sisters. Their choir prayers are the Marian Office (*Tageszeiten*). The choir sisters are all well educated and come from well-to-do families. The lay sisters come from the lower, working class, very often unable to read or to write. These lay sisters take care of the heavy work, but the choir sisters also are busy throughout the day with work and teaching. They do not keep a boarding school (*Pensionat*), but they instruct poor children free of charge. They also visit the sick in pairs and bring aid to the poor. They bring medicine to the sick and clothing to their children and provide pious (*heilsame*) instructions, etc. etc. At noonday many poor people come to them to get something to eat. They have a large room on the main floor. One sister prays with them and gives them a short instruction (*Unterricht*) and then gives them food. The funds for the upkeep of the convent come from the capital that the choir sisters bring with them on entering. The lay sisters need not bring a dowry with them on entering. These 'Sisters of Mercy' have found a rapid acceptance (*verbreitet*) in England, Ireland, Scotland and America. Wherever there appears to be the least need the 'Sisters of Mercy' will be found. In Birmingham, for example, I was astounded by how imposing their institution was. There was hardly any need for a contemplative order in Ireland. The present Archbishop of Dublin, Cardinal Cullen,[5] has introduced the Redemptoristines as in England. Earlier, Carmelite nuns existed in New Ross in the south-east part of Ireland, who, however, were obliged to teach school. When the Redemptoristines came to Dublin, the Cardinal Archbishop ordered that they were to live strictly according to their rule.

I said earlier that the Catholics lost most of their land to Protestants. Land usually belongs to noble families, as it does in England. The nobility has several grades, beginning with the royal princes and dukes, then come the earls which we would normally translate as counts, but an earl is usually more than a count with us. There are also marquesses. The ordinary nobility starts with lords and then come the knights and the baronets. They are the same as our barons. The lords are hereditary members of the upper house of parliament. In order to become a lord landed property is necessary. It is consequently not possible to be a lord simply because one's father was one. He has to have inherited the father's property. The feminine of lord is lady. The children who do not inherit the property are known as 'honourable'. No division of property takes place. All property goes to the eldest son, who is then responsible for keeping the substance of the family intact. Other children receive something, which is usually not sufficient for their upkeep. A place, therefore, has to be found for them in the church or the military or the civil service. This refers to nobility 'with title'. Now there are also people who are considered nobility and have no title, or, as they are called in England, 'gentry without a title'. These men and women are little different from the bourgeoisie (*Bürgerliche*) except that they have landed property. At home we call them owners of lordships (*Herschaftsbesitzer*). In the English language they are preferably called 'gentlemen'. In England, Ireland, etc. much importance is attached to being born into a good family (*Abstammung*). Only property can legitimise a title. There is a substantial difference between a title with wealth and one without. Peasants who are property-owners are very few. The landowning 'gentleman' has his estate (*Grundkomplex*), his castle and his park with peasants' dwellings around it with the usual land attached — all part of his property, which he leases out. Consequently the peasants are usually leaseholders. Protestant landowners in Ireland do not like to deal with Catholics. Therefore they lease the land in large parcels to so-called middlemen and often consume their income in England or on the continent. In this way the money leaves the country. These middlemen then rent out the land in small parcels to the people. The poor people are therefore trapped. In England the people can work in factories; not so in Ireland. They have to rent a parcel at any price whatsoever in order to survive. Consequently they remain very poor. If they cannot pay their rent, they are simply turned out. And what do these people do when they are put out on the road? They live so miserably in respect to food and clothing that our people at home could not imagine it.

Instead of bread they eat potatoes. Because of a lack of change of clothing, they are full of vermin. The day-labourers and other workers live just as miserably. The poor nutrition results in bad stomachs, which they then try to cure with whiskey. It happens frequently that one drinks whiskey to get so drunk as to forget, for a short time at least, one's misery. This is the reason for the drunkenness of the Irish. All good alcoholic beverages are imported at such a high tariff that they are completely out of the range of the common man. That leaves only 'whiskey' (that is what spirits made of grain is called, which is frequently adulterated with unhealthy spirits made from potatoes). This whiskey they produce frequently in secret so that they will not have to pay the excise tax.

There was a Capuchin, Father Mathew,[6] in Cork, in the south of Ireland, who preached temperance, which was nothing but an imitation of the Protestant temperance societies in North America. The Irishman is by nature endowed with a lively temperament. He is very passionate in love and hate, in friendship and in enmity. He allows himself to be driven by his impulses and only later reflects on them. Father Mathew had huge success, but it was only temporary, because he lacked the necessary foundation, i.e. prayer and the Holy Sacraments. Father Matthew [*sic*] earned such a great reputation as a result of his supposed success that Queen Victoria assigned him a £400 yearly pension (*gehalt*).

The poor nutrition did not allow enough energy for work, and the Irish were unjustly accused therefore of laziness. I was told the story that in the north of Ireland a Scotsman leased a farm, i.e. a peasant holding (*Bauerngut*). He hired some Irishmen and told them what work he expected of them. They said that they could not carry out his request. He then said: 'I know that, but listen, I will give 1 shilling a day for 14 days without your having to do any work except the condition that you buy food with it every day, and only after that will you be asked to begin working.' In this way the Scotsman nourished the famished Irishmen, and then they worked harder for him than he required of them. These people cannot even think of saving anything. Consequently they are in a depressed state. They do not think of improving their land, because the only result would be higher rent.

In spite of the fact that the Irish were a martyred people and their Church had been very much damaged, in time a reform was absolutely necessary. As far as my experience is concerned, I know that a people whose religious life has decayed can never reform itself. Reform has to come externally, especially from Rome. The present Pope Pius IX therefore sent a reformer to Ireland, who was himself an Irishman and who was raised and trained in Rome. He was a personal friend of the Pope even before the Pope was elevated to the papal throne. This was the present Cardinal Archbishop of Dublin, Dr Cullen. When the Archbishop of Armagh, the Primate of Ireland, died, the Pope selected Dr Cullen as Archbishop of Armagh and appointed him at the same time *Delegatus sedis apostolicae* [Delegate of the Holy See]. As such, he immediately convened a national synod. The Bishop of Limerick[7] later told me the bishops were not convened to make decisions but only to listen and assent because Cullen brought everything already prepared. The English government planned at that time to establish higher schools of learning for Protestants and Catholics in which also Catholic professors were to be appointed. The offer was enticing and well arranged. There were clerics and priests who wanted to accept the offer, but the synod would not endorse the government's plan and the professorships offered were forbidden to Catholic clerics. The archbishop, Dr Cullen, was also designated by the Pope to supervise all the religious orders in Ireland. He ordered that the dress of the order had to be worn at all times in the house as well as in the church, and he removed all the female servants from the monasteries and thus restored order. This was no easy task. After the Archbishop of Dublin died the Pope translated Dr Cullen to Dublin with the title of *Delegatus sedis apostolici* [*sic*], as a result of which he took precedence over his successor in Armagh despite the fact that the latter was the Primate.[8]

Paul Cullen had great influence over the selection of bishops. When a bishop dies in Ireland, the parish priests of the diocese meet to select a successor. They propose three names for this honour to the Pope, *dignissimus*, *dignior*, *dignus* [most worthy, more worthy, worthy], from which the Pope selects one. While I was in Ireland there were cases, however, where the Pope ignored them all and chose a person recommended by Archbishop Cullen. In the liturgy, also, Cullen proved himself a complete Roman, which was necessary. As a result of this intervention, he was considered by many a *persona ingrata* [unwelcome person], which did not bother him at all. He was not a man with many pretensions; he was affable (*leutselig*), but he gave the impression at all times of an aura of great authority. With the Irish as with the Tyroleans, the Pope is in principle everything. But they are deeply nationalistic. And if one tries to reform them, they demur as do the Tyroleans. The Tyrolean believes that simply being Tyrolean is being a good Catholic, and so do the Irish: being Irish is being a good Catholic. In Belfast, a large city in the north of Ireland, there was a bishop who was a strange fellow (*komischer Kautz*).[9] He was an antagonist of all the regulars. He opposed the establishment of a convent for the 'Sisters of Mercy'. Thereupon Archbishop Cullen established the convent with a chaplain in spite of his opposition. In Ireland not far from Dublin on the railroad line to the west there is a Catholic institution called Maynooth, where the Irish priests are trained. This college receives subsidies from the English government — but why? Earlier the Irish clergy were educated in Paris. The government did not like this and wanted them to be trained at home, as a consequence of which annual subsidies were approved by parliament. But the clerics who are graduated from Maynooth are often more scholarly than they are pious. In addition they receive a monthly stipend. Consequently those who come from this institution take on more the airs of 'gentlemen' rather than becoming apostles to the poor. They are more critical than pious about their theology. With most this French rigorism is only superficial. This makes the [pastoral] workload lighter, so that one has more time for complaint. The proverb holds meanwhile: *nulla regula sine exceptione* [there is no rule without an exception]. I found in Ireland many of the small works of St Alphonsus translated and published, and also examples of great respect for St Alphonsus. [. . .]

## *II. Limerick*

We began our mission in Limerick, where the bishop, John Ryan, a good man, allowed us to do good things, but in other respects acted entirely in the tradition of Irish clerics. What follows is typical of him. In the house of the Christian Brothers he and his clergy made their *Exercitium*, or retreat. But he could not understand why complete silence should be observed. He thought that clerics should be able to talk to each other. Nevertheless, he submitted to the regulation. Limerick has 50,000 inhabitants, of whom 10,000 are Protestants[10] and 40,000 Catholics. There is also a Protestant bishop in the city who occupies the beautiful old cathedral. The newer, more beautiful part of the city is predominately inhabited by Protestants, the older and worse part by Catholics. The city is on the River Shannon and is about 80 English miles away from the western coast. The sailing ships come up to the city. The part of the Shannon below Limerick actually represents an 80-mile-long ocean inlet into which the Shannon flows. For that reason the sailing ships are able to reach Limerick. In the Catholic part of the city the place is full of children, testifying to God's grace in giving the Catholic Irish great fertility with which they populate England and the other provinces. Wherever they go, priests follow, churches are built, and eventually dioceses are formed. And wherever they go their heart always remains in Ireland. Because there is freedom to marry, there are no illegitimate children, and the confessional retards the *fructatio proli* [*fructificatio prolis*, the bearing of children?]. We also found a number of empty houses in Limerick. This is the result of migration. I found in Limerick three Catholic parishes. St John and St Michael were the bishop's mensal parishes, that is, the bishop is the parish priest and receives the income and keeps his vicarage there. He does not have a cathedral church of his own. He lives at the edge of the city in a park. In the city there was a Franciscan and a Dominican convent. There was also a convent of the Good Shepherd nuns in which there were about 80 female penitents (*Poenitentinen*). The superior was a German from Munich, the daughter of General Balligand.[11] In her youth she learned Latin and Greek and was as fluent in Italian, French and English as in her mother tongue. The entire institution was still in a very primitive condition. Everything was in a utilitarian way well appointed, but the building was damp. The superior was a good-hearted woman with an energetic and soldierly manner. I often worked here apostolically. These ladies thanked us for this and provided us with many kindnesses. There was also in Limerick an imposing institution of the Sisters of Mercy, also 'Presentation' nuns and a cloister of the nuns of the Sacred Heart with a large number of boarders (*Pensionat*). Also the Christian Brothers had a large institution here with several schools.

The first churches built since the persecution were actually makeshift churches without any style, with a small bell in the steeple. They liked them in the form of a cross †. Where the beams crossed was the altar, which was approached by 5 or 6 steps, so that the priest could be seen by everyone. From there one could also comfortably give a sermon, so that a pulpit, even if one existed, was superfluous. Behind the altar was a sacristy and above it frequently a choir. The choir consists always of an organ and singing. In all of Great Britain and Ireland I never heard instruments used in the church. At the end of the cross-beams there were galleries. Churches that were built later were similar to those built here [Austria]. If the church was not cruciform †, then it was merely a large hall. Then there were galleries on three sides and the altar on the fourth. The galleries and the space near the altar were reserved for those who paid an admission fee and made voluntary donations. The rear was reserved for the very poor. As in England so it is also in Ireland, there is a separation between those who have something and nothing, since the latter are usually full of vermin. Moreover, the upkeep of the bishop, the priests and the church depend on the revenues from admission fees and voluntary offerings.

St John's Church, in which we held our first mission, was built in the form of a †. The church stood in a courtyard and was separated from the street by a wall. The part of the city in which the church stood was rather dirty. Quarters were rented for us nearby in Clare Street in a house owned by the Good Shepherd nuns, which was empty because its occupants emigrated. They put some poor furnishings in it. The vicar arranged to have us cook and eat by ourselves. There were four of us missioners. I, Father Petcherine, Father Van Antwerpen and Father Douglas. Father Coffin and Father Furniss were at that time still in the novitiate in Belgium.

Father Douglas and Father Petcherine came from Clapham to Bishop Eton. Our good neighbour Mr Sharples[12] made reservations for us on the steamship to Dublin. When we left, I was out of sorts because we were going to hold missions in a country about which we knew very little. I was supposed to organise the missions there, but first I had to orient myself. Father Petcherine was more of an enthusiast *in dulci jubilo* [in a joyful shout], which does him honour. He viewed the Irish as a poor, persecuted people and since his youth he has identified with them. I, however, had already met Irish people in America and England. I liked them, but at the same time I recognised several of their shortcomings. And it was these that caused me concern. Before we departed I called the Fathers together and told them how much the Irish like 'whiskey' punch. I told them that the Irish are accustomed to it and therefore can take a great deal of it. We on the other hand were not used to it, and it could easily happen that a missioner could get drunk at a social gathering. Therefore we will promise (*vorsatz*), i.e. not an oath, not to drink whiskey. They all agreed, and this promise was kept at all times and as long as the mission was under my supervision. It was only in Letterkenny that I made an exception for myself, which I will explain later.

The trip from Liverpool to Dublin was overnight and took eleven hours. The sea was rough and demanded its tribute in seasickness.

Only Father Petcherine did not have to pay. We landed in Queenstown [*Kingstown, now Dún Laoghaire*], which is actually a harbour for Dublin for the steamships. It is a new city, and it is a short railroad journey to Dublin. After we arrived at the Dublin railway station I saw a sign on which it was written in large letters that if a railway employee takes a tip, he will be dismissed. Dublin is a beautiful city with 200,000 inhabitants. Besides Queenstown [*sic*] there is another large harbour that serves the city. The streets are beautiful, but the many ragged, poor people considerably impair this good impression. We stayed in Dublin only a few hours; at ten o'clock we left by rail for Limerick. I observed that in everything the Irish were trying to imitate the English, but that they would not succeed. The country through which the railway went was not interesting. It may have taken us three to six hours. We travelled by 2nd class. In England 2nd class is for common people and late arrivals, and it is only in trains that make all the local stops that one finds a third class. In Ireland all trains have a third class, therefore 2nd class is for a better class of people. As we arrived at the miserable station in Limerick we saw the bishop getting off the train as well. He had travelled first class from Dublin. We were not acquainted with him, but given the circumstances we realised he was the bishop and requested his blessing. He immediately invited us to dinner. The clergy of St John's were also there to greet us and we were introduced to them, and after hearty greetings they escorted us to our quarters and from there we went to dinner to the highly esteemed bishop. Dinner was very simple and only water was drunk. Dinner took about half an hour, and then the whole party went into the other room. Here were the whiskey bottles. Whiskey was poured into jugs and warm water was poured on top and the jug placed next to glasses with small spoons. Here the bishop and all those present made themselves punch, as weak or strong as they wished. We too were invited to partake, but we thanked the bishop and said that we wished to abstain. The bishop was a bit disconcerted over this, but immediately ordered some Spanish wine for us, which we drank. The conversation was pleasant.

On the next day, a Sunday, we opened the mission. I always arranged it so that the opening should fall on a Sunday at the regular church service. I always considered it very important that the people should hear the opening sermons, because that is the reason for the whole thing. A mission in which the congregation has not heard the opening sermons is like a building without a foundation. If the people are to hear the opening sermons, it is advisable that they should hear them in the church that is familiar to them to encourage their further attendance.

In all of Ireland the late service on Sundays begins at twelve noon. But I arranged that it should be announced for eleven o'clock. We missioners walked to the church from our house with the biretta on our heads. At the door of the church the clergy welcomed us *more solito* [in the customary manner]. I did this only twice, once in the cathedral in Liverpool and the other time here. I was very sorry about this because the circumstances were not of the kind to create a decided impression. It is not the honour of the missioners but the impression on the people that is the real purpose of such ceremonies, which have to be well prepared and well acted out, otherwise they are of no consequence. The Irish clergy were used to doing everything *brevi manu* [using the short form], dispensing with all ceremonies. Before I ascended into the pulpit the bishop came out of the sacristy attired in mozzetta and stole and sat down in a specially prepared armchair in the presbytery. He did not have a throne. His appearance caused a sensation among the congregation. This made me realise how highly the Irish honoured their clergy. After I requested the bishop's blessing I ascended into the pulpit and began my introductory remarks. The order of my presentation was as follows:

1. What is a mission? It is a sermon of the Word of God through the words of human beings.
2. Where do we find this Word of God? From the Church of Jesus, which with the help of the Holy Spirit is infallible. This is the Catholic Church, and why? This Church has presented the Word of God in a small book, which is called the catechism.

3. We are preaching nothing new, therefore, but something very ancient. Even though we instruct, we do not do this because we believe that you are ignorant. We produce evidence (*Beweisen*) not because you are unbelievers, for we know that in your souls you are good Catholics. Our purpose in these lectures is to look at the Word of God so that your hearts will be totally saturated with it, because to have the Word only in one's head helps little. We do this for several days in a row, like a blacksmith with his red-hot iron until the job is finished.
4. The truths that are to be transmitted are of a double nature: sour and sweet, bitter and pleasant, etc. But the sour and the sweet form the foundation. First of all we must learn to fear God. Then we can build love on top of that. We are not allowed to exaggerate anything, nothing should be sharper or harder, nor easier either, because both would be false to the Word of God. And when we preach about Hell, it is in order to avoid the road to Hell and find that to Heaven.
5. Another purpose of the mission is that we settle our account with God in accordance with God's peace so that we can die as children of God and enter into a state of bliss. The way that we achieve this is that we compare our past life with God's laws and to beg forgiveness for any transgression.
6. Out of this comes the importance of the mission for the sinners, the lukewarm and the good. This task must be well and totally accomplished.
7. The rules that are to be obeyed demonstrate that everything depends on God's grace. Therefore prayer and appeals to the Mother of God are necessary, etc.

This introductory sermon I find to be necessary everywhere, but especially for England and Ireland. There are those who travel about and give lectures and organise conferences etc. etc., which people attend in droves out of curiosity. Consequently it is necessary to tell the people what the purpose of a mission is, and often this sermon is also necessary for the bishops and the clergy. After that I offered the High Mass *de Spiritu Sancto* [of the Holy Ghost]. In later missions we omitted the ceremonial reception of the missioners. I arranged the Masses on opening day so that a missioner read Holy Mass at the altar every hour. After the reading of the Gospels (*Evangelium*) the missioner made an appeal to the people. In this way we wanted to replace the so-called *Sentimenti* [exhortations] that St Alphonsus required to be proclaimed publicly in the streets the day before the mission. At 11 o'clock the introductory (*eingangs*) sermon was presented and then the High Mass *de Spiritu Sancto*. Later we had to take the *missa de festali* [saint's festal Mass] because I was told that a mission was not recognised by Rome as a *causa publica* [public reason] for a *missa votiva solemnis* [Solemn Votive Mass]. We did not return for the noon meal until 1.30 p.m., if not actually at 2 o'clock. After that there was nothing until the evening. We began the Rosary at 6.30 p.m. There was no sermon with it, as is the custom in the Tyrol, but according to Italian custom as St Alphonsus required. Then followed instruction in the catechism. This gave me trouble because no one had been prepared for it, that is, the person who undertook this task during the mission and the instruction in the catechism that was connected with it [was not prepared]. Therefore I had to give different parts of the catechism to different people. It was consequently a patchwork and not what St Alphonsus prescribed. If one person were in charge of these instructions and if he discussed with the pastor the needs of his congregation, then he can take a short cut and spend more time on the important things. Much time is gained in this way and the whole thing can be accomplished. This will not work, however, when the material is divided among individuals. [. . .]

These instructions were always incompletely carried out because of the lack of preparation. Somebody has to take complete responsibility for the missions. It requires much study, experience and knowledge of people. I had nothing but novices. I also had to give most of the important sermons. Father Petcherine was an experienced preacher, but he broke down no walls. He was very much loved because he was completely suffused with love for poor children and often publicly praised them. This [attitude] might lead him to neglect (*ubersehen*) certain things. In short, he did not preach with the necessary seriousness and energy. He was very lovable. Moreover, I was so constantly chased from one task to another that I also lacked the time to study the popular catechism. I had one person who promised to become a good popular catechist, Father Van Antwerpen, whom God, however, took away through death. Not all people are suitable for this task. Long sermons are easier and take less preparation than the popular catechism. We do not understand how important this insight is. This is because one holds fast to the traditional errors and does not study the precepts of St Alphonsus concerning missions. One reads here and there, but no one does a thorough study. And consequently we make all sorts of mistakes on our missions and therefore we are not able to harvest the fruits that they should bring. Because we were poorly prepared we often had to give general conscience-raising sessions instead of catechesis. After the catechism (*Kartechen*) there was an *intermezzo ad relaxandam mentem* [intermission for the relaxation of the spirit] either by singing a song or through a holy blessing . [. . .] Then followed the main sermon, which we held late at night. [. . .]

The following day, very early in the morning before the working day began, we had a Holy Mass and meditation. [. . .] Here too we experienced great shortcomings, because for these observations it requires special talent and preparation. The best preachers are often not up to that task. The mission to children, which later played such a large role, was totally omitted from the first mission in Ireland, because we first had to orient ourselves, and besides we lacked Father Furniss, the children's missioner. Despite the many shortcomings and mistakes in our missions, we tried to do our best to correct them in order to organise our missions according to the precepts of St Alphonsus. From time to time a certain vexation took hold of me against my superiors because they left the training for the missions to those who carried out the missions etc.

As soon as we began to hear confessions, the confessionals were literally surrounded by penitents. What eagerness the people demonstrated might be shown by the following. I ordered the sexton to open the church at 4 a.m. Once he opened the church at that hour and found a large number of people already around the confessional. He was surprised and asked how they got in. The answer was through the window. The people had cut the glass out of the window, which could be raised. They then found the nail inside that was there to prevent the window from being raised and took it out of its hole. Then they raised the window, and all went in through it. Our hearing confession in the morning and at night gave the people an opportunity to confess, because many did not have time during the day. After they confessed they went to communion. In that way we also gave the priest a good lesson. We took people as they came without distinction. We made no distinction between the well-off and the commoners, between the rich and the beggar, the well-dressed and the ragged, the well-educated and the uneducated. The people soon learned that we drank no whiskey during the mission and accepted no invitations, that we sacrificed ourselves to the poor and to the sinners with love. Consequently they honoured us with the name 'holy fathers.'

This dedication was not easy. It required that we overcame the smell of the ragged and the all too visible vermin that moved on their clothing. Every day when we returned home from hearing confessions we had to search our clothing for vermin. The lice were unusually large, so that they brought us to the point of wanting to vomit. As a rule we slept only 6 hours. About noon we usually had 3 hours of respite, including our meal. Whoever wished could take a brief nap at this time to ward off the desire for sleep during the hours in the confessional. The rest of the time was devoted to prayer and to studying for the lectures. I allowed the Fathers to have a little wine at their noon meal. My superiors, however, forbade this later. There were some Fathers who maintained that wine was a luxury in Ireland and complained to our superiors. Some did not want to eat fowl either because they thought it was forbidden according to the rules. I had my cross therefore with such people. The superiors should have first consulted with me rather than having taken decisions immediately after the complaints. In Ireland it is often easier to get fowl than beef or veal. We gave up all distilled spirits anyway, but to forbid wine after all our hard work I thought was going too far. Thereupon they allowed us a little wine after a meal, if anyone was so inclined. The drinking after a meal I found very awkward, but I submitted to it.

I have gone into considerable detail here because this mission was a model for all other missions in Ireland. Differences and changes and unique elements I will mention later, as far as I can remember them. We kept to the habit of eating by ourselves, which did not cause us any difficulties. We found this to be self-evident.

I am not sure how long this first mission in Ireland lasted — certainly more than fourteen days and possibly three weeks.

St Alphonsus says one should remain in one place until the work is done. At this time our work was not even half-way complete, but what should we have done? Others took care of our meals and our needs. In this way I began to worry whether we were causing too much trouble. At any rate, I decided to break with this procedure, for I felt how important the rule of St Alphonsus was that we ought to take care of our own needs. Because there was a large space in the church reserved for the poorest, I was not aware of the question of the evil of entrance fees as I was to be later. We received an honorarium four or five times our travel expenses, which I naturally liked because I needed money for my house in Bishop Eton.

Now a few particular things. About one hour from Limerick on the River Shannon towards the sea there was a large noble estate with considerable holdings whose size I have forgotten. Its owner's name was Mr Monsell.[13] He and his wife were fervent Protestants belonging to the Anglican high church. He was very anxious to convert his servants and his tenants. In this he was successful with his coachman and his housekeeper. The lady of the house is not in charge of housekeeping. The housekeeper was in charge of the female servants. The lady of the house enters the kitchen only rarely. The coachman too is among the top echelon of the servants. He does not work in the stable nor with the wagons. He does nothing but drive the carriage, and if his lordship or others of his household want to travel, the other servants have to take care of getting the horses and carriage ready. Once everything is ready, the coachman mounts his seat with white gloves on and has a servant hand him the whip. Mr Monsell also wanted to convert his tenants, who were all Catholic. For that purpose he called them all together at one time and had his Protestant pastor demonstrate to them what nonsense it was for them to pray according to the Litany of Loreto. As soon as this name was mentioned all the peasants cried out 'Pray for us.' He realised that he could not succeed and thereupon said to his pastor: 'Let's go home because these people pray to the Mother of God just to spite us.'

This Mr Monsell himself converted to the Catholic Church. The more detailed story of his conversion is unknown. Now that he was a Catholic, he was as fervent as he had been as a Protestant. As far as my experience goes, I believe that fanatical Protestants are easier to convert and become much better Christians than the indifferent ones who act nice and sweet in everything. That is the way that his wife acted. She was Lord Dunraven's sister, who had his own properties in the neighbourhood of Mr Monsell. She remained a Protestant. He tried to get the coachman and the housekeeper back to Catholicism, but they refused. Mr Monsell came often to our sermons. Finally I was told that his wife would also come. This was the right time, because I had just the right subject for her. Because the Protestants complain that we have too many ceremonies, which put Jesus Christ to one side, I wanted to demonstrate how all in the Catholic Church recall Jesus and His martyrdom. She really did come, and I waxed hot on my subject. I thought that I had made a good impression on her, but I was wrong. Mr Wilberforce,[14] also a convert, told me that her impression was negative. 'Everything was fine', she is supposed to have said, 'but why did the preacher not encourage his listeners to read about the martyrdom of Jesus in the Gospels? What is clear from this is that the priests do not want to have the people read the Holy Scriptures themselves.' I answered that I could have easily fulfilled her wish, but who can think of everything?

This Henry Wilberforce was the son of a great statesman and speaker in parliament who thought to bring about the freedom of thought and the abolition of slavery.[15] He had 3 sons, one of whom became the Protestant Bishop of Oxford and died in this position.[16] Another became a dignitary of the Protestant high church, converted and was ordained a priest in Rome, and died on the way home to celebrate his first Mass.[17] The third [Henry] was also rector of a Protestant parish church, converted with his wife and children and thus lost a rich sinecure. He inherited estates from his brother, however, in the islands of western Ireland. He writes a great deal in the 'Catholic Standard' for the Catholic Church.

In this mission we planted a cross for the first time in the courtyard of the church. The cross without the Christ figure (*ohne Christus*) was made of oak. The consecration was done one Sunday during services. I said High Mass at 11 o'clock, then we went in procession to the cross, where the consecration immediately took place. After we were seated Father Petcherine gave a nice fiery sermon. He was a master of that kind of sermon. The Catholic elite of Limerick were also present. It was a truly heartrending triumph. This mission was the reason for the desire that we should have one of our houses (*Kloster*) in Limerick. Mr Monsell was a great supporter of this project. The Franciscan Guardian[18] came to speak to me in the sacristy. I was greatly surprised when he appeared in a frock coat, stand-up collar and a neck-cloth. He confessed and later came to Bishop Eton to make his retreat. The end and the veneration of the Mother of God occurred *more solito* [in the customary manner] with great participation on the part of the people.

After this mission Mr Monsell invited us to relax for a few days on his estate. We accepted this invitation and travelled by boat on the Shannon accompanied by Mr Wilberforce and several other Catholic 'gentlemen'. We were also cordially received by his Protestant wife, who placed a Bible in every one of our rooms, a fact that made us laugh heartily. Dinner was at 7 o'clock in the evening. Mr Monsell had a chapel in his castle (*Schloss*), with the privilege of having the Holy Mass said and to receive the Holy Sacraments. In this chapel every day there is a one-hour devotional service where quite often the Litany of the Blessed Virgin is sung, to whom since his conversion he had special devotion. His wife, the coachman and the housekeeper did not attend these devotions. As much as he opposed the Litany of Loreto while he was a Protestant, he loved it that much more after his conversion. Prior to dinner we assembled in the 'library'. That is what the living or reception room was called. His large collection of books were placed in open stacks for general use.

When the butler announced dinner, Mr Monsell asked me to take his wife in to dinner. This is an honour for the chief guest. According to the custom of the country, I was supposed to give her my arm and thus escort her to the table. This even the bishops do, and I saw Cardinal Wiseman[19] do it. I was very embarrassed by this request. I approached the lady and told her that I had never given my arm to a lady and that she should excuse me and I proposed that we walk side by side. We indeed went into dinner together, and the rest of the company followed us. The following evening Mr Monsell did not ask me to do this. On this occasion and several others I felt a deficiency in our training. We had not been instructed in the ceremonies of the country. This appears to me to be essential for a missioner in our day. One looks very inept and it is as if one lacked good upbringing, like a peasant. The judgement of people about the training of a missioner has important repercussions in regard to his usefulness. The Jesuits excel in this respect. They know how to behave in company, whereas we often demonstrate a lack of understanding for the rules of good behaviour and are therefore often censured, and consequently we are not as effective as we might be.

There are among us those who pride themselves on this kind of behaviour. In our training and studies we have been instructed through readings, oral observations and conferences, with the examples taken from the old monks and the hermits; but our life is fundamentally different from theirs. As long as the holy Ignatius Loyola lived by himself, he was a complete monk and hermit of the ancient type. But as soon as he became active as an apostle, he carefully observed all the rules of good behaviour and sensibility. As a matter of fact, all the saints were far from being coarse (*Derbheit*). In their humility they were courtly and decent (*Hoflich und anstanding*). St Paul himself says: *omnibus omnia factus sum ut ea Christo Crucifaciam* [I have made myself all things to all men in order that I might crucify those things for Christ]. Consequently a missioner should understand and observe the ceremonial so that he does not offend people but will instead win them to Christ. Our constitutions require this, and it is exactly in these things that our Fathers should be instructed. It is unfortunate that we were not trained thus, and, as a matter of fact, damage resulted to the good cause. Because of that, those who were self-educated in these matters also went too far. Therefore the Prefect of the 2nd Novitiate should be a well-educated and experienced missioner. At least, that is what happened to me, and I had to try out things without sufficient preparation. And I observed that it was also the case with others.

Now I will mention in my story how one particular day when Holy Mass was being celebrated very early in the morning in the house chapel, Mr Monsell was both sacristan and sexton. He confessed and took communion while his Protestant spouse was still in bed. At 8 o'clock we had a big breakfast (*Gabelfruhstuck*). The Fathers thought that it was overdoing things to eat and drink like that so early in the morning. They only drank their coffee and ate some bread with butter. But they had to suffer considerably for this. I, on the other hand, greatly enjoyed my breakfast. After this large breakfast an excursion into the country was organised. We inspected the ruins of a former abbey. The walls of the church and even the stones of the altar were still standing. Mr Monsell asked us if we did not want to rebuild the abbey. Naturally I had to decline. I said the old walls would have to be torn down and new ones built, because the old walls had remained without a roof for so long and exposed to moisture and decay. Then there is the problem of the upkeep of the community, I said. The old monks used to have a great deal of property, but we have neither property nor capital (*Capitalien*). In order to exist we would have to live within a large population. He well understood this and was even more interested in helping us establish a house in Limerick. At about 2 p.m. we arrived at the mansion of Mr Monsell's brother-in-law, Lord Dunraven,[20] who unfortunately was not at home. So now we were faced with the problem of how we were to secure something to eat to keep us until 7 o'clock in the evening. You will not find any inns here like at home. There are, to be sure, pubs (*Schenken*), but they are so common that no 'gentleman' would dare to enter. One may imagine how hungry the Fathers were. The next day they ate their big breakfast with great gusto.

This Lord Dunraven, or rather the Earl of Dunraven, was outwardly a Protestant, but in his heart he was a complete Catholic. He would very much have liked to convert to Catholicism, but he had been told that such a step would kill his wife, who had heart disease. To compensate, he refurbished the Catholic church near his mansion and brought brothers and nuns to teach in Catholic schools there. I do not know what happened to him later.

Mr Monsell's marriage was childless, and his entire property would go to Protestants. I learned later from Mr Monsell that they were very determined Protestants from northern Ireland. But God took his Protestant marriage partner to Himself, and he then married a good Belgian Catholic. God placed this convert too in a very visible position. He was repeatedly elected to parliament and even became a member of a ministry and thus was counsellor to the Queen [member of the Privy Council], where he acted, thought and felt as thoroughly Catholic as at home. He continued to be an initiator and supporter of our establishment in Limerick.

What we did after this mission I no longer remember. I did not keep a diary, and everything that I am writing down now depends on my memory. We journeyed often between England and Ireland. Since there have been many interruptions, it is very likely that I may repeat myself inasmuch as I do not recall the chronology of all our work. Whatever I remember and observe I write down. One mission that we convened without children was in the cathedral of Liverpool. The parish clergymen, precisely those whom Father Buggenoms[21] thought would join us, did not. They were the ones who talked me into making the opening ceremony in the same way as we did in the Tyrol. I wrote out the entire ceremony, but it turned out to be a disaster, and therefore I determined in principle that it should never be done again.

We heard confessions here every day until midnight because the people had to work during the daylight hours. They would lose their jobs if they missed one single day. How long this mission lasted and how many Fathers there were I do not recall. We could also send people to our house in Bishop Eton for confessions. I want to report only two things about this mission. The parish priests told me about a person who apparently went to confession in order to tempt the priest hearing the confession. I had similar cases earlier. I understand such women go especially to younger priests and tell them all sort of nonsense which they never did in order to tempt them. Based on my earlier experiences, I believed what the priests told me. Because the priests already knew her, they asked me in God's name to watch out for who she went to for confession. I have to mention here that the confessionals were actually confessional booths (*Beichtkammen*). We literally caught her as she was ready to confess to Father Vanderstichele and threw her out. I also know of a case in which a priest was able to clear up (*aufklärte*) a difficult situation with a young lady. She had gone to [another] priest and confessed that she was in love with him. He [the first priest] asked her if they [she and the second priest] had discussed anything carnal (*unkeusch*) in the confessional. She said, yes. The result was a *denunciatio* [by the young lady of the second priest] to the bishop. Instructed by such cases, the bishops decided not to pursue such instances of denunciation. Such [episcopal] intervention should only occur when two denunciations were made against the same priest. It is sad for such priests when the women understand how they can take revenge on them.

[*Pp. 140–154, which are omitted here, are not concerned with Ireland and deal mainly with Prost's experiences on the continent.*]

I wanted to visit Trier, where the Reverend Father Poesl was building a house and a church, before I returned to England, but all of a sudden I received a letter from England that his lordship the Bishop of Limerick requested that I conduct a second mission there. While I was absent in Koblenz our people conducted smaller missions in Armagh and Londonderry in the north of Ireland. I travelled swiftly to Ireland in order to begin the second mission in St Michael's Church, the 2nd mensal parish of his lordship the bishop. We held it in the same way as the first mission, only a bit longer and at 11 o'clock Mass there was always a sermon *pro nobilibus* [for the nobility]. We lived at that time in a house on Bank Place, which Mr Monsell rented at Father Held's[22] request. We organised a chapel in the house. This house was to be the beginning of a permanent establishment in Limerick. In the meantime it was to serve as a resting-place to recuperate from our work in Ireland. In my efforts to furnish the place, the Good Shepherd nuns were very helpful. At that time deliberations were going on concerning the selection of a good place for our house and monastery. Three places were suggested. I opposed the first because the surroundings were too dirty. The clergy favoured it because it was a place where there were poor people. I answered that the poor people could come to our house and our church, which need not be in such a place, etc. The second location was too far outside the city. The third location was where our house and church now stand. That place, however, was at the time not available. This was the period when the Shannon docks were being built, and the landowners were speculating with their real estate. This speculation proved to be a chimera, and as a result the location became available. In the meantime everything else remained in *status quo*.

Because of the business of our settlement in Limerick, I came often to that city, even after several missions. On such an occasion the following happened. It was at 11 o'clock on a Sunday and I was looking out of the window and saw a sizeable mob approaching. In the middle of the mob I saw two men going arm-in-arm being jostled by the people. This whole scene appeared to me as if a buzzard was flying overhead with swallows attacking it all the time. I thought that these two men must have done something to embitter the people.

While I was seeing this and thinking about it a priest came and enlightened me. The Protestant mission society of England, he said, all of a sudden had dispatched a hundred preachers to Ireland to go into the different cities and to hold meetings in the streets simultaneously on the same Sunday to mobilise a turbulent mob against the Catholic Church.[23] Ten came to Limerick, and each went to a different part of the city and mounted banks or barrels and harangued the crowd.

As soon as the people realised what their purpose was, they became angry and the entire city was in an uproar. The preachers found themselves heaped with insults and had to retreat. One of them would have been tossed into the Shannon if a Catholic priest had not rescued him. This was the story the priest told. Later I found out that even the Protestant Bishop of Limerick[24] was alarmed by this uproar. He declared that these preachers had done these things without his knowledge and that he knew none of them. The mayor of the city[25] summoned the preachers and accused them of causing a disturbance and requested them to leave the city immediately. He told them that he would provide sufficient police to accompany and to protect them as far as the railway station. But the preachers said that they would prefer to have two or three Catholic priests rather than policemen as protectors; they said that they would feel safer with the priests than with 160 policemen. Their request was granted, and thus they went to the railway station under the protection of the priests. The preachers experienced the same result with minor variations in the other cities. Consequently the entire effort of the Protestant missions in Ireland came to nothing. On the contrary, the people showed even greater attachment to us.

I have already expressed earlier my concern over the small number of crucifixes in the Catholic churches of Ireland. Therefore I took a number of crucifixes from our rooms with me to Limerick. There I told a painter to make black polished crosses and to attach alabaster-like white Christ figures and to place them in his store window. As a result, people stood in front of this store window all day long to admire the crucifixes. I also gave him the address of the Belgian merchant who procures these crucifixes from the Tyrol. In this way I was able to provide this man with considerable business, and thus crucifixes became the norm in Irish churches and homes. We also took such a crucifix around on our missions and set it up on the pulpit. We also carried with us a large picture of the Mother of God by Murillo. I had it put on a linen canvas and hung in the churches in which we gave a mission. We also took with us a wooden crate with a chalice, a ciborium, ostensorium, censer (*Rauchfass*), vestments, etc. etc., because many churches were indeed poverty-stricken.

I have to repeat here that I try to tell things in their chronological order, but that errors will creep in, because I did not keep any diary and must now rely on memory for everything. For that reason I am unable to give the exact year for all matters.

Once in Limerick I heard that Dr Cahill[26] and the apostle of temperance (*Massigkeit*), Father Mathew, were in the city. I wanted to meet them both in person and therefore looked them up. Father Mathew had unfortunately left the city, but Dr Cahill was still there. The latter is a priest who travelled around the country giving lectures on electricity, astronomy, etc. He did this in order to defend the Catholic Church against the Protestants. And in fact he became a hammer much feared by the Protestants, but was on account of that highly celebrated by both Catholic clergy and laity. He was very kind to me and especially indicated his pleasure at our mission. This Dr Cahill promised to give a lecture at the request of the bishop to the children of a female convent school where 70–80 sick children lived.[27] They wanted him to lecture on optics, acoustics, astronomy and electricity. I was well known at that educational institution because I held a retreat there for the nuns as well as the children. But Dr Cahill could not come because of a conflict. Consequently the bishop asked me to replace him. I accepted the task and arrived at the appointed hour. All were curious about what I was going to lecture on. At the beginning I expressed my unhappiness that Dr Cahill, who was such an expert and such a scholar, could not be present. I wanted to assure them that I would at least try. I began with the science of eyesight and pointed out that true sight was only possible through faith. Then I went on to the question of hearing and asserted that true hearing was to hear the Word of God. Then I demonstrated that their view of Jesus on the cross should electrify their hearts. Then I came to astronomy and declared that the stars were actually the saints. They should try during their life to emulate the saints. This lecture came to be discussed throughout the city, both humorously and seriously. The children too reported it to their parents. Dr Cahill said that these lectures were better than his own.

*[Pp. 161–164, omitted here, give an account of the departure of Frederick de Held from England to Belgium.]*

As I am writing this I recall that Father Furniss had already been active with his children's mission at the 2nd mission in Limerick, because the parish priests were somewhat upset as he allowed the children to approach the sacraments too quickly. [. . .] I can no longer remember all the details about the children's mission in Limerick. I want to say only that the children's mission of Father Furniss appeared to me as a novelty. But because St Alphonsus writes about it, I was willing to let it go on. Soon, however, I recognised the great good that it accomplished and gave Father Furniss a free hand. Father Furniss was totally devoted to his work. The rector who followed me at Bishop Eton[28] thought one ought to break Father Furniss's head (*Kopf brechen*). But I cautioned him against this before my return to Germany. I said: 'What Father Furniss does is very good and enormously useful. That his entire soul in involved in this work is very helpful to his achieving his goal. If they take this task away from him and break his vocation, then they will destroy everything. Is that better? As superiors they are his father and they should help in his devotion to his work, and thus they would help him achieve complete salvation, and this way mitigate his weakness. If they order him to do something legitimately, then they will preserve his calling and all the good that he is doing in rescuing the souls of the children for the honour of God and the Congregation.' The rector followed my advice, and thus Father Furniss died after achieving a number of apostolic works, true to his calling as a Redemptorist.

I can also recall that Father Furniss worked very hard and successfully at the children's mission that was part of our mission at St Anthony's Church in Liverpool. He also instructed the children in the practical way of listening to the Mass. In St Anthony's Church in Liverpool there was an altar, which was hidden by a movable wall while school was being conducted, and was opened when Mass was said. The children were assembled for Sunday services. Father Furniss made an agreement with a parish priest that he should say the Holy Mass there. Then Father Furniss explained the different parts of the Mass to the children and said some very short prayers. He tried to encourage the children to become especially devoted to the Mother of God, the Child Jesus and the Guardian Angel. He had them come to confession twice, and only after the second time did he allow them to receive communion. Not infrequently on such occasions was the Holy Sacrament of Confirmation offered. Father Furniss had his detractors, but Cardinal Wiseman and Archbishop Cullen answered those detractors. [. . .] I was even more surprised when I was told that at one of our General Chapters one of Father Furniss's opponents made a case against him, one who should have known better since he was himself an eyewitness to what was Father Furniss had done. Sadly, there are those among us who are not willing to tolerate things that do not accord with a correct point of view (*schönen Kopf*). It is exactly these opponents who interest themselves more in the exterior brilliance of the mission. As far as I am concerned, I can say before God, even when the mission was most brilliant, that was not what I had in mind; furthermore I never thought it had to go according to my desires, but that I only intended that everything should go according to the rules of St Alphonsus.

Once we also held a children's mission in St Patrick's Church in Liverpool. This church is so large that the ground floor could hold 7,000 children. In addition the church had on three sides large galleries. The main floor was used only for the children and was always full. The adults were allowed to use the galleries, which were also always full. Father Furniss did not participate in this children's mission. I do not remember why. Two Belgians, Father Vanderstichele and Father Theunis, took his place. Father Vanderstichele was able to imitate Father Furniss's manner completely, and Father Theunis supported him splendidly. The lectures were held after the children left the factories. We began with the Rosary and ended with the sacramental blessing. On Sundays both in the forenoon and the afternoon the sermons were on the duties of parents. Confessions were heard until midnight. Ten priests took part in the work. Each priest took a group of children and examined them to find out if they knew what was necessary. With some who were not well prepared he would have to give additional instruction. To the most accomplished he gave 'tickets' which they had to show at the confessional booth and at communion. Those children who worked in the factories received their Holy Communion early in the morning, the others received it later. All received a short preparation or homily (*Vor bereitung*) and an expression of thanksgiving. This was an enormous task and lasted four weeks. The sacrament of Confirmation was offered twice and sometimes three times. After four weeks we had to stop because we were totally exhausted. We terminated the mission with the hope that we would continue it at a later time. The children exhibited an extraordinary zeal. The children themselves became missionaries and brought others to the mission. The children's mission made a deep impression even on the adults, especially the parents.

We did not lack malicious people who wanted to make trouble, but the parish priests were able to prevent it by being alert and energetic. A convert who was not yet a priest was a great help in this respect. He came from a rich family that had ostracised him on account of his conversion. He taught the children a short song about the Mother of God. This man did his best to give the mission more life. He sang the *Ave Maria Stella* every evening, and after each verse the children accompanied by the organ sang the refrain to the Mother of God. The children sang this refrain in the streets as well. Many abandoned children became real Christians in this way, and many eighteen- to twenty-year-olds made their first communion and were confirmed. I cannot remember all details of our work. I want merely to explain how we came to hold these missions at our own expense and how we did it.

Charging admission to the sermons in the church was always a thorn in my side. But what could we do? Our living and travelling expenses had to be paid, etc. Consequently one has to permit the parish priest to collect the means to do that. I insisted that the poor people should be allowed to enter without paying. This was indeed promised. For the poorest the church did offer places without charging admission fees. But there were people who did not belong among the poorest and who could not be expected to associate with the poorest because they were infested with vermin and who were ashamed of their condition. Those who needed the mission the most, that is, people who neglected their souls, were not willing to pay anything and, moreover, attended at best only on Sundays. Others did not have the means to pay an entrance fee for all members of their families for every day of the mission. Consequently it happened that one family member came to one sermon and the others did not. There were also other problems. I finally came to the conclusion that some used the missions simply for making money (*Geldmacherey*), even if it were for good purposes.

## *III. Ulster*

At that point the parish priest of Enniskillen in the north-west of Ireland requested a mission. He did not write to me but to Father Buggenoms, who was at that time the superior at Clapham. Father Buggenoms requested that I provide the mission. I asked him to postpone the mission for the following reasons. Though Enniskillen was no large city, it was the headquarters (*Hauptsitz*) of the Orangemen, who were Freemasons and the most determined foes of Catholics. It was exactly about the time when new elections for the English parliament were being held and which were connected with the fiercest fights especially in Enniskillen.[29] I thought that it was very awkward to hold a mission at such a time and in such a place. Moreover, we missioners were at the time completely exhausted and required a short rest. But what I have often observed also happened here. Those who always remain at home and do not participate in any missions have no sympathy for the harassed missioners. In their ignorance many see the constant travelling of the missioners as entertainment. Father Buggenoms answered me roughly that if I would not do the mission, then others would have to be found to do it. Nevertheless, the mission was postponed, at least for a little while.

We then journeyed from Liverpool to Enniskillen for the mission. Father Coffin and Father Furniss and others participated. Enniskillen is located on a lake in a very pretty area. We occupied the quarters of the curates (*Kaplan*), who in the meantime lived elsewhere. The parish priest lived near Enniskillen in a country house.[30] We were astounded at the poverty of the church. It had no sacristy, only a trunk near the altar in which all the wherewithal for the Mass was stored. The church was low and the altar small, with a torn picture above the altar. The church was dirty, and one could see here and there cobwebs. Our first task was to dust, clean out the cobwebs and sweep the church, which every one of us did. I ordered that Father Coffin act as church prefect. He fashioned a sacristy next to the altar behind some curtains, where we stored our church things which we had brought with us. We covered the torn picture and replaced it with a picture of the Mother of God that we had brought for devotions and put the crucifix that we had brought on the altar. The Catholic people looked extremely miserable, even pitiable. The wealthier were the Protestants, etc. etc. I asked the priest to introduce us next day to the people. He arrived in a dress coat and a black neck-piece and a so-called 'father-murderer' (*Vatermörder*), i.e. a white starched collar. Thus clothed he ascended the steps of the altar. There was no pulpit. His introduction was hardly different from one in which 'gentlemen' are introduced in a social gathering. The unusual thing at this introduction was the request for money from the people. As an example he related that at a mission in Londonderry, in the bishop's church, £200 was collected. I was standing near the altar, and I felt like sinking into the floor. I then gave my opening sermon. As poor as the church was, as nice was the new Catholic schoolhouse. In it Father Furniss with Father Vanderstichele performed with astounding success. The poor Catholics came out of their holes and came into the church.

The Protestants, especially the Orangemen, were astounded by the mass of people who came to church. They had not expected such crowds of Catholics, and they began to be fearful. From this one can draw the conclusion that the interest in going to church had not been especially strong. Protestants and Orangemen came to hear us preach. They thought that our only aim was to attack them. When they understood that we were peace-loving and mainly wanted to impress upon the Catholics that they should cease drinking, stealing and swindling, etc. etc., they left us alone and allowed us to work without hindrance. The Catholics here had never seen a ceremony, a benediction, or a censor. Because we had brought everything with us, we had benediction every evening. Father Coffin and Father Van Antwerpen were good singers. Everyone was astounded at by this. We also held an exposition *(Aussetzung) Sanctissimi* [of the Blessed Sacrament] for 2–3 hours. Father Coffin took care to have it especially well-lighted. I was astounded at the devotion of the people. We erected here, too, in front of the church a mission cross. While the mission was going on, the bishop of the diocese[31] came to visit the parish priest. I cannot recall whether he came into the church. The priest invited me to dinner, together with the bishop. Here I understood that the priest was not a 'gentleman.' I was treated in a flattering way. The very honourable bishop was especially friendly, but I was displeased because I could not understand how the nice living quarters of the priest could be squared with the miserable and stable-like (*stallortig*) condition of the church. In spite of that, the people still retained the highest respect for such priests.

I can no longer recall how long this mission lasted. When we left, there were twenty-one converts who were registered in the parish register. Most likely there were others after we left. We departed in two separate groups. I no longer know the reason for this. I, Father Furniss and Father Coffin were in the first party. We went to Londonderry in order to open a mission at the 'Waterside' in a newly erected church.

When we left Enniskillen, the whole area around where we boarded our carriage was full of children who said goodbye to Father Furniss. The children were so enthusiastic that we had trouble getting to our carriage. The driver had to go very slowly because the children were all around the carriage. Many accompanied us for a good distance, and we had great trouble in urging them to return. What one could make of such people if they only had different priests!

The distance to the railway station where we took the train to Londonderry was not far. There we were welcomed by the priest of 'Waterside', who took us to his house and turned it over to us, and he found quarters elsewhere. The next day we were given the newspaper of Londonderry in which there was a story about the arrival of three popish priests, Prost, Coffin and Furniss. It would have been better to put Prost into the Coffin and throw him into the Furniss. [. . .] Truly a pleasant welcome. Nevertheless, we were left in peace. As I did earlier by letter, so I negotiated now by word of mouth that the people should be allowed in without an admission fee to sermons etc. He promised to do that. He was an eager priest, already forty years as a saver of souls (*Seelsorger*), totally different from the priest in Enniskillen. The church was on a nice rise opposite the city. The river, or rather the ocean, was between the rise and the city. The church had a roof, but was not yet finished on the inside. The city was called Maidencity, i.e. virgin city. James I, the son of Mary Stuart, made a gift of the entire district to the city of London, hence the name Londonderry. Before that it was called Derry. The city of London forced the Catholics out and brought in a Protestant population. Thus the whole city became Protestant.

James II of England, as the Duke of York, was a Catholic and as such ascended the throne after the death of his brother, Charles II. Both were grandsons of James I. Their father, Charles I, was overthrown as result of the Cromwellian revolution and was decapitated in London. The son-in-law of James II, William the Prince of Orange, deposed James II. The Irish took up the cause of their Catholic fugitive king and were on the verge of capturing Londonderry. Thereupon a Protestant preacher fired up the people to defend the city, and it could consequently not be captured. Hence the name Maiden City. A law was enacted preventing any Catholics from living in the city. This law was in force until the Emancipation of the Catholics. Catholics had to live outside the city walls. The first Catholic allowed to live inside the walls was the rich, respected Mr Mehan.[32] His children told me that a mob formed itself when he settled in the city. His wife and children had to flee to the rear of the house so that they would not be hit by stones. He was allowed to remain in the city, and the city reimbursed him for all damages. Thus a few Catholics came to live in the city. The 'Sisters of Mercy' established here an imposing institute. After the other Fathers arrived much courageous and fruitful work was done.

How long this mission lasted I do not know. We attempted at all times to carry out the rules of St Alphonsus and to remain as long as was necessary, *in quantum potuimus* [in so far as we could]. After all, as long as others took care of our upkeep, we had to work accordingly. What I feared also happened here. They tried to collect money from those who came to the sermons. Indeed, some were not admitted into the church unless they paid. As a result, I was very depressed. I began to grumble in my innermost being against the superiors in that they could find no other means to defray the expenses of the mission in order that all could come to our preaching without having to pay and that we would not have to be forced to shorten our missions. I began to wish we had not purchased the house in Bishop Eton. I said: we should have kept Hanley Castle and Great Marlow and thus have saved £6,000 sterling to use for missions, how much good could have been done, etc. etc. I began to complain that one had money to buy expensive things for the church but nothing for missions.

Had I known then how much money was lost on speculative ventures instead of using it for the missions, I do not know what would have happened. I thought about how our superiors like to preen themselves by reminding their subordinates concerning the rules of St Alphonsus. Why do they then forget completely his rule concerning the expenses of missions, which is to be found in the text of the rules as approved by Pope Benedict XIV. That one could carry these rules out the following will demonstrate. One praised the good things that the missions accomplished despite the fact that this rule is not obeyed. It is true that much good has been done, but how much more would have been accomplished if this rule had been observed. One should rather think of the good that cannot be accomplished and the harm that is done to the souls, precisely because this rule is not obeyed. I said once at a conference in Bornhofen that St Alphonsus had immeasurably fewer means than we had and nevertheless observed this rule. At that point the rector became angry and said 'this is the business of the superiors' and thus broke up the conference. In the General Chapter (*Generalkapitel*) in Rome in 1855, according to a 'vocal' who told me himself, 'they go about holding "Consulta" on money matters, when they should also hold "Consulta" concerning the health of the souls'.

At this mission a beautiful mission cross was erected in front of the church so that the entire city could see it. His lordship the Bishop of Londonderry honoured the mission with his presence at the festivities.[33] Cripples and sick people were also brought to receive the holy blessing from us. Such was the strength of the faith of the people. I definitely know of some who have been healed. Many have received relief. During the mission I was shown a place in the valley where the Catholics used to worship secretly, also a shed (*Schupfe*) near the river which they used as a church. The priest, who had been in office for forty years saving souls, had never held Benediction *cum Sanctissimo* [with the Blessed Sacrament]. We had to instruct him.

How long that mission lasted I do not remember. The Mehan family, of whom I spoke earlier, had a country house on the same Waterside, lower down near the harbour and immediately across from the city. On that spot there once was a famous convent of St Columba. A wall of the church was still standing, and even the Protestants have great respect for it. The popular opinion is that when a property-owner takes a stone from it, he will not be a property-owner much longer. They recall the invariable experience of this family after the father had died. His widow was still alive. This couple had three sons and two daughters. One daughter joined the Ursulines in Cork in the south of

Ireland. The other was still living at home, but she too wanted to become a nun. But in order to take care of her old mother she did not go through with this decision. The eldest brother carried on an extensive business. The youngest brother started his career as a lawyer. All three are bachelors. The eldest wanted to marry, but just before the wedding his [proposed] bride joined the 'Sisters of Mercy' in Londonderry and at the time of the mission was already professed. The second brother also wanted to get married, but his [proposed] bride decided to join the Ursulines in Cork and had already been accepted.

This family invited us to their place after the mission was over for rest. We accepted their invitation. They had a very nice chapel with the wherewithal for the Mass. It had been the room where the father died. We lived there as comfortably as we did at home; in the evening we were expected for 'Diner'. There were usually guests present, because this family was among the first families in Londonderry, if not the very first. I have reported once already that in Ireland 'whiskey' punch is served after dinner. Because it was known that we refrained from drinking any, none was served in our presence. But as soon as we left the company the punch-drinking started. We usually went to the living-room, and sooner or later the ladies joined us there and tea would be served. There was there a wonderful 'fortepiano'. Father Coffin is a master on it. We chanced to talk about the 'Maselliaise' [*sic*], and I said that I had never heard it. Father Petcherine and Father Van Antwerpen volunteered to sing it, and Father Coffin accompanied them on the 'fortepiano'. Now I understood the effect that this song could have on people. The text and the song is really overwhelming. One has to say that some portions of the text are certainly correct in their meaning; for the great and powerful were in recent times so horrible that they excited anger and abhorrence in the people. In the history of the pagan church one can expect nothing else; but when such things are found in Christian lands, as the history of the recent centuries demonstrates, then the heart has to rebel. The Christian people have endured and suffered much, and that these people, led by the example of the great ones, should become unbelieving and rise up against their traducers and oppressors is only natural. Consequently God sent a Napoleon, who whipped them around (*herumpeitschte*). But the great ones have not learned anything, or very little. What will come to pass?

Once the Bishop of Raphoe[34] in Letterkenny was a dinner guest. Raphoe was in ancient times a city with a bishop west of Londonderry. Now Raphoe is a poor village and the bishop resides in the nearby small town of Letterkenny. He begged us to give a mission in his church in Letterkenny. I agreed to come, but with the condition that people would have free admission to all sermons and lectures, for which I also gave him my reasons. He agreed to see to it that all the poor would be admitted free and without hindrance to hear the Word of God. I was also satisfied, and we agreed to the time of the mission.

In the meantime Christmas was approaching. I wanted to celebrate Christmas with my subordinates at home. Father Petcherine and Father Furniss remained with the Mehan family, and I, Father Coffin, Father Van Antwerpen and Father Vanderstichele shipped out of Londonderry on a boat to Liverpool. The captain and others on the ship treated us with all possible care. At approximately one o'clock we boarded the ship, and towards four o'clock we were in the open sea off the northern coast of Ireland. A powerful storm developed at that time and did not let up until Liverpool. In this storm we had to travel between Ireland and Scotland under constant danger to life and limb. Even the captain was afraid at times. Our people at Bishop Eton knew that we were coming and had great fear for us. We arrived 8 hours later than we were expected. We celebrated Christmas together and very pleasantly. We had a very good piano. Brother Stephan was a good player, and Father Van Antwerpen etc. etc. sang the most beautiful hymns. The services were also held in a festive manner.

After that we went to Letterkenny for the mission. We picked up the priests whom we had left in Londonderry and went to Letterkenny, where his lordship the bishop took us into his own house.[35] He retreated altogether into his parlour and left the entire house at our disposal. The house stood in a large garden, or rather a large meadow, which also contained some trees and abutted the churchyard so that one was able to go from it to the sacristy behind the altar. The church was surrounded by a large wall. The church was built according to the old Irish style in the form of a cross † with three galleries. The church had only one altar with five or six steps. No more were necessary because the bishop had only one priest, who was his cousin and his successor as bishop. His name was MacGettigan.[36] In the church there was no throne for the bishop. He sat in the first chair on the Gospel side. He can be likened in every way to a rough Austrian village priest. He was able to behave himself, if a little crudely, in polite company, but that is how Pope Gregory XVI and King Louis Philippe liked to see him. There exist a number of droll anecdotes about him. He welcomed us very cordially and said: 'Now you priests must share with me some "whiskey" punch.' When I told him that we abstained, he was somewhat surprised but admitted that his clerical cousin was also a 'temperance man'.

As everywhere, with few exceptions, we also dined here by ourselves. We began the mission, and I went around the church to see if there were any money collectors. I saw none and was therefore happy. But on the second day Father Furniss and Father Vanderstichele came to me and told me that money collectors stood along the fence of the churchyard. Then I had to hear reluctantly that some poor people had to climb over the wall of the churchyard and one girl broke her foot in the process. I do not recall any more what the occasion was by which we had the women go into a gallery. When the bishop came into the church and saw this, he thundered and threatened with his cane, so that everyone took flight out of the gallery. But how did the bishop keep his word that he gave me in Londonderry? Quite well, according to his opinion. When he announced the mission, he also proclaimed that all the poor should come to him to receive admission tickets without charge. Naturally most people were afraid to go to the bishop for fear of hearing all sorts of harsh words from him. As I said earlier, many are not so poor that they are unable to give anything at all, but not rich enough to give at every service and for all the family members on every day. Consequently many absented themselves. There are also those who could give but do not wish to give anything to save their souls. The great sinners, for whom the mission is the most necessary, should be given incentives to come. But when admission is charged, they will not come at all. That was like a thunderbolt for me. But right away I requested that Father Coffin make preparations for a humble apology (*Abbitten*).

Father Coffin knew how to make such arrangements very well. He made a bishop out of the bishop, that is, he constructed in the *Sanctuario* [sanctuary] a seat for the bishop and decorated the altar in a fashion that had never been seen in Letterkenny. He clothed the bishop like a bishop. But he allowed him only to assist from his seat for the ceremony and the sermon. The entire ceremony was by ourselves. I preached and showed the love of Jesus for us in the Holy Sacraments and how our sins and our errors are opposed to this love. In the course of my sermon I turned to the wealthy Catholics and reproached them for showing so little love to Jesus in the Holy Sacraments because they would not support the bishop and his priest sufficiently and the bishop and his priest were forced on account of that to such an 'abominable' recourse as to have money collectors at the fence of the churchyard. I said bring forth your voluntary offerings, then the bishop and his priest can allow the poor to come and hear the Word of God and to pray to their God through the Holy Sacraments, etc. etc. But they understood very well that the sermon was really meant for the bishop, because they did not like the money collecting during the mission. The bishop sat there in a horrified (*erschrocken*) state. As the preacher I recognised his embarrassment. The church was chock-full, especially of the better people in the community. Everyone was affected. The whole was concluded *more solito* [in the customary manner]. The bishop went immediately to the sacristy and took off his vestments and hurried to his house. I thought that I should pursue him right away so that the storm could be dissipated immediately. I caught him at the house door. I said to him: 'My lord, I am so exhausted, I could stand a glass of "whiskey" punch.' He answered: 'That you shall have.' He went himself into the cellar and got up an old 'whiskey' and mixed the punch and gave me and himself a glass of it. We sat in a brotherly way and drank our glass without mentioning one thing about what had happened in the church. The result was that the money collectors disappeared and the mission went on well, but at our departure he gave us no money for the trip.

After this experience Father Furniss gave me a sum of money in order that I could begin to finance the missions myself. He offered me £200 sterling out of his *patrimonium* [inheritance].[37] I accepted his money and immediately travelled to Omagh, where the next mission was to have taken place, while the mission in Letterkenny was still going on. Here I organised everything accordingly with the priest. I took care of all the expenses for travel, upkeep, etc. The parish priest offered his house and his servant for the duration of the mission, and because it was too small for us, a Protestant neighbour who was also a Freemason was willing to rent out a few rooms. His wife was Catholic and so were all his children. This Protestant and Freemason was rewarded by God for this service of love, since he converted to Catholicism, not during the mission but shortly thereafter, causing a considerable stir. The parish priest was going to live with a Catholic family for the duration of the mission. This was a temporary benefit to him because he ate and drank without having to pay and in his own house he had no expenses during the mission. He obligated himself also to turn over everything to me in the church and the sacristy during the mission. As a result, I was placed in the position of allowing all to come to the mission without charging entrance fees. Because there was still a separation between the better-off classes from the poor, for the reasons mentioned above, I decided that those who wanted to go to the galleries would have to pay a token one penny. Then I wanted the collection plate (*Klingelbeutel*) to be circulated after the catechism instruction and before the sermon. We would keep everything that was collected in this way, except that on Sunday all was to go to the parish priest. The priest was satisfied, and I made this arrangement the rule during all the following missions that I directed.

After I had arranged everything I returned to Letterkenny in order to finish the mission there. I cannot recall completely how long the mission there lasted, but I think it was four weeks. After the money collectors disappeared the attendance considerably increased. Father Furniss and Father Vanderstichele did wonders with the children. The rest of us worked with the adults. As elsewhere with the missions, we had to work here against a secret society, which purported to be Catholic: I mention it at this point because we had here an especially brilliant success. This society called itself 'Ribbonmen'. Ribbon is a silk ribbon, which they carried as a distinctive mark. This society may have been totally innocent at the beginning. Catholics created them as a protective device against Protestants, who constantly oppressed and harassed the Catholics. They overreached themselves, however. This society went so far as to hold a secret trial for the specific oppressors and persecutors of Catholics and decreed their punishment. Those who were to carry out the punishment were chosen by lot. The punishment depended on the transgression and could include arson or other material damage and sometimes even murder. Those chosen to execute the verdict had to fulfil their charge if they did not want to be subject to the revenge of the society itself. This society could be found all over Ireland and England, but we noticed that it was especially strong around Letterkenny. This society was strictly prohibited by the bishops, and its members were excommunicated. Our mission made such a strong impression on the members of this society that they came to us in masses and abjured their membership and accepted the Holy Sacraments. Many swore on my mission cross. In the end we were able to bring to the bishop the insignia and diploma etc. of a Freemason who converted. At that point the bishop began to weep. 'I have been a bishop for thirty years, but I never experienced such a conversion.' As soon as the mission was over, the leaders of this society came to reconvert their fellows but without success.

One of the fruits of this mission was the entrance into our Congregation of a son of one of the better families of Letterkenny. I have forgotten his name. Following this mission we went to Omagh, where I had already prepared everything. Our Fathers had already worked here before, but this was the first formal mission. The mission also lasted four weeks. I appointed the worthy Father Coffin bursar. He was too much the 'gentleman', however and made an agreement with the innkeeper concerning our meals. I understood that this was unworkable. We suffered financial losses. I kept this entirely secret; if our superiors had heard about it, our mission would have been cancelled. At the next mission I appointed Father Douglas the bursar, as I will relate below. Our mission in Omagh was in everything excellent. On this mission we recruited the very worthy Father Harbison for our Congregation.[38] He was a priest belonging to the diocese of Armagh. He came to see us and begged to be admitted. I sent him to Bishop Eton in Liverpool for the time being in order that he could make his exercises under the very worthy Father Lans and to test his vocation etc. He then returned and is now a very useful member of the Congregation. While I was in Koblenz Father Petcherine worked with one or two others in Omagh and enrolled people in the Scapular Society. The following occurred there. A father who was enrolled in the Scapular Society had a very unruly son. The father lectured his son with all his power. Thereupon the son swore to revenge himself on his father. Once both went to church to hear Holy Mass. The son kneeled behind his father and during the consecration of the Host (*Wondlung*) he took his knife out and put it in his father's back. The knife, however, went only as far as the scapular and no further. Naturally he was apprehended immediately and turned over to the court. And while we were still in Omagh on the mission there was a trial in which the scapular was used as evidence. I do not recall what happened to this murderer of his father, but the incident awakened in the Catholic populace a surprising devotion to the scapular. I wanted to make use of this experience in the following way.

The people receive their wages for the week on Saturday night. Many then go directly to the public houses and drink part of it up. Some of them become drunk and go home and begin to fight, which results in scandal. On Sunday they are sick and cannot come to church, and their family suffers for the rest of the week, etc. etc. A missioner naturally has to devise methods to counter this. At that point I came to think of the great veneration in which the scapular was held. I have to mention here that the scapular generally comes from Mount Carmel.

The enrolling in other kinds of scapulars was only an exception for individuals. I began with the principle that with such things the people should also understand their significance and that their *multiplicitas* [proliferation] among the masses would hinder this understanding. I explained the significance of the scapulars to the people and invited them to put themselves under the protection of the Mother of God. I also explained all the requirements that the Church prescribed in order to gain these privileges. Because they did not fulfil these requirements, the Church gave us the power to exchange them into good works. I then said given this power of proxy I will now change these requirements as follows: 1st, that they abstain from spirits on Saturday night. 2nd, that from Saturday night to Sunday night they visit no low bars (*Schenken*), but hotels and regularly licensed inns are not included, because they do not tolerate the so-called drinkers or drunkards. Our [Austrian] life with inns is here unknown. These bars were places where one congregated to drink spirits. 3rd, that once a week they were to recite the Rosary. They could do this by dividing the devotion up over the entire week. I explained to them that none of this was sinful. The observer would gain, but the non-observer would not be sinful, though he would not have the benefit of wearing the scapular piously because one declares thereby that one will attempt to become a Child of Mary. I had another reason to insist that only the Scapular of Mount Carmel was permitted. The people either had to make their own scapular or have it made for them. We were unable to carry such a large quantity with us. We could not have given them the scapulars gratis. And if we took payment, then malicious people would accuse us of being in business. The Scapular of Mount Carmel required only two pieces of brown cloth with two strings. This the people could easily acquire.

An unbelievably large number took this scapular with the requirements that I prescribed. The effect was wonderful. There was such a bar right next to the church. Normally on Saturday night it was full and lively. Now the bar was empty and the publican stood in front of the door and read the newspaper. I was tremendously happy about this. Wives and children were also pleased because the fathers brought home their full wage. But my happiness was short-lived because our good work was forbidden. And who was responsible? Our own superior. Some complained that I was trying to introduce an innovation with the scapulars. Following the complaint came the prohibition and a request that I explain my action. And I was the loyal donkey who followed orders, which I still regret. I should at least have objected because the cure of many souls was involved. I had been trained to obey, and with sorrow I must say that there are superiors who do not obey the rule *audiatur et altera pars* [let the other side also be heard] and who adopt a certain attitude of infallibility. And thus they misuse the blind obedience of their subordinates.

## *IV. Wexford*

Our next mission was in Gorey, a village with a church on the east coast of Ireland south of Dublin, a one-day trip. There was a large simple Gothic church with a large rectory and a convent and an educational institution of the Loretto nuns, which with us are the so-called English ladies. Everything was arranged as in Omagh, except that I appointed Father Douglas bursar and our meals would no longer be brought from the inn but would be prepared in the house. Even though we were able to cover all our expenses, we received here more than we paid out and were thus able to eliminate our deficit in Omagh. The people wanted at first to push delicacies on us. I rejected it all and told them that if they wanted to give us something, they should give us bread and meat, etc. That would be fine with us. Thereupon we received bread and meat, etc. etc., so that we had to purchase very little. If we had done our cooking in Omagh, the people would have brought us everything and we would not have had any losses and instead would have made a profit (*Profitiert*). The parish priest came to me several times and gave me £1 sterling, with the plea that a Holy Mass would be said for him. He too wanted to contribute something to our mission. At the end of the mission I publicly thanked him for this. Our willingness to sacrifice and our unselfishness became known all over the country. We were even more admired because we rejected all invitations. We remained here three or four weeks. Over time the enthusiasm of the people grew, and also the collections. During the mission a funeral service was held for a rich person to which the very reverend bishop and all the priests in the vicinity were invited. Every priest received £1. We also were invited, but we declined because it would interfere with our obligations in the confessional. That too increased the people's respect for us. This gave me additional courage, and I reported it to my superiors. Father Held knew how to appreciate this and even permitted the Fathers of Clapham who came to me on the mission to receive my views on how the holy mission should be conducted, for which I paid their travelling expenses.

Thus we finally achieved our goal: to organise the mission as St Alphonsus prescribed. The fears concerning the costs of the missions disappeared. Only I and no one else knew how much a mission cost. The fact that we were able to pay for our own missions increased respect for us immeasurably. We were in a position to continue the mission until our work was finished without any outside support, exactly as St Alphonsus stipulated. In that way we gained three benefits. (1) we had time or we gained time not only to throw fear into the people but to preach God's love, (2) we did not need to pile on sermon after sermon so that all the people could hear them and digest them, (3) we needed fewer missioners, which reduced transportation and food costs and made it less difficult to find lodging for the missioners. When the mission lasted longer, fewer missioners were required.

Since we gave our sermon in the morning before work and in the evenings after work, nobody missed any work, except on days of confession; and because we heard confession late into the night and gave communion early in the morning, the parishioners did not lose any work time even on that day. Everyone who wanted to could hear all our sermons. Because the missions were longer and because we did not discriminate according to class in hearing confessions, the priests were always free in relation to granting absolution. One could take care of the penitents even before absolution and do the appropriate thing. Moreover, all haste was unnecessary. How were we able to do this? Because we made the mission self-sufficient and we lived by ourselves. No other way was possible. Without this 'arrangement' the disorder in our missions would have been impossible to resolve. If this 'arrangement' were not so terribly important, St Alphonsus would not have insisted on it. As I am writing these memoirs I discover that the Jesuits used the same methods in their missions in the Tyrol before they were suppressed by Clement XIV. With our 'arrangement' the bishop was willing to tolerate our mission, because the priest had to turn over the church and the sacristy only for the duration of the mission. He was able to stay in his house comfortably and without interruption. When the priests in Omagh and Gorey turned their houses over to us, they did it voluntarily. In addition they benefited. They lodged with some well-off parishioners and thus saved the costs of their own upkeep. And because they lodged elsewhere, they had no expenses in respect to hospitality. Only in these two cases did we live in the priest's house. In the other missions which were conducted in this way, I arranged for the lodgings. Father Held advised me always to proceed to the place where we planned to be and arrange everything in advance myself. There I myself searched and arranged for accommodations. With this 'arrangement' the priest had no excuse when the bishop wanted to have a new mission. All excuses fell by the wayside because the priest could not say that 'I do not have the means or any room in the house for the missioners', or that 'the people will lose time from work'. Even the poverty of the church and sacristy could not be used as an excuse, because we carried all that was necessary with us. The priest's rights are thus carefully respected. And especially when the priest is unco-operative about the mission, it is the most necessary. We cannot force the priest to accept the mission, but the bishop can and he has frequently been obliged to do that duty.

Here I have to discuss the complaint of some of our Fathers that formal missions are useless etc. It is true that it is an evil when the priest does not want such a mission. It is unreasonable to expect from such a priest that he help the mission. This is an evil, but it is wrong to say that such a mission is useless etc. How many confessions that are invalid (*Gottesräuderische Beichten*) are made good in this way? How many will be converted and lead at least for some time a good life? And even priests who do not want to have missions are thereby taught better, and if they do not allow themselves to be taught quite often, they become timid and cautious in front of their flock.

When the mission members live together with the priests, the mission is often damaged. We have our own weak spots and mistakes, which the priests soon become aware of when we dine with them. Unpleasant priests soon learn to exploit these things. Then there are those who make a scandal out of every little thing. How difficult is it for a missioner to live together with a priest under such tension for a long period of time. [. . .] Count Chambord had a mission arranged for Lazarists near Frossdorf where he was requested to pay 5 gulden per missioner per day. The prince had to pay 1,000 gulden.[39] Only recently we were asked to pay 400 gulden to a priest so that he would not be out any money. Naturally under such conditions one has to terminate the mission as soon as possible. The work is done too fast and is incomplete. Thus the mission bears no fruit and loses credibility. In short, the cost is the *punctum puncti* [the real point], and without this no real reform is possible.

Should we not be able to do what the much poorer St Alphonsus did and what we were able in the much poorer Ireland to do? For the past forty years our Austrian province has lost 100,000 gulden in speculation. In Trier our confrères gambled away 10,000 taler[40] in six months. What resources did we have? I was the head of a house without capital and without a fixed income and which on top of everything else depended on the goodwill of the house at Clapham for every penny. And despite everything, we brought it to the point where I was able to carry all expenses, and that even in the poor Ireland. This could happen even more easily in Austria. Why is it not done? No one thinks of it, and, indeed, every one becomes nasty when one talks about it.

The priests, it is maintained, will be unhappy when one does not live and eat with them. This can easily be negotiated. Moreover, for the greater good one should be willing to put up with some unpleasantness. On the contrary, priests have already told me that they did not oppose a mission; they only wanted to have peace and quiet at home. Good insightful priests see the failings in the missions and sigh and lose all confidence in them. The bad-willed ones are made smart by the devil, so that they see all the mistakes and exploit them to oppose the missions. The missions no longer have the attraction of novelty about them, and they must earn their credit through their intrinsic value. But many among us do not want to listen to any talk of reform and on the contrary become annoyed when one talks about it. I said: there are many who agree with me but do not dare say so. [. . .] It is complained that the missions have little or no content. That is true, but we are mostly to blame. Those who understand this are silent, following Eccli 32, 6, *Ubi auditus non est non effundus sermonem* [If you are not being heard, do not waste your words].

It is wonderful how God has blessed us with mundane means since the year 1820. Our superiors have not made bad use but good use. We have provided a good example in that we have beautified churches, procured costly vestments and other equipment for religious service, have elevated religious service and advanced the reception of the Holy Sacraments, etc. etc. Even that is to the credit of the Congregation. One must recall that the superiors have used the funds for the existence and growth of the Congregation. Because they did not want to use these assets to pay for the expenses of the missions as St Alphonsus has prescribed, therefore, it appears that God has shown his displeasure in that our temporal speculation was not only not blessed but He allowed it to fail with great damage. Through that our temporal as well as our eternal well-being has been damaged and also the missions which are our real vocation. What I mean is that if we had used even ¼ part of our temporal resources for the missions, we would even in our temporal resources be better off. The honourable Father Hofbauer gave a perfect example of how it should be done. As soon as we follow his and St Alphonsus's example, our Congregation will blossom.

[Notebook III, pp. 1–30]

In the previous notebook we stopped with the mission in Gorey on the south-east coast of Ireland. I have to add the following concerning this mission. In Gorey there is a workhouse which takes in many who would otherwise die of hunger. But there are also people who are compelled to enter this workhouse, i.e. those who are itinerants. These workhouses are really penitentiaries, from which the inmates are not allowed out into the world even if they went in voluntarily. They are forced to work, which is good, but the men are separated from their wives, and children from their parents. Their nutrition is minimal. The poor are deathly afraid of these workhouses and enter them only at the point of starvation, some even preferring death from starvation.

These workhouses are the creation of the Protestant English government. As long as the Catholic spirit and Catholic charity lived and reigned, they were unnecessary. The monasteries and religious foundations took care of the poor in a paternally loving way. Only after the elimination and destruction of these institutions was it necessary to think of such workhouses. The monasteries that are rising again in England and Ireland reduce the hard lot of these people, but their means are insufficient to take care of them all.

Where Catholic associations have been entrusted with this task, the lot of the poor is much improved. But the Protestants and the liberal Catholics who think the same way can help only with the aid of the secular authority, which is usually tyrannical and kills the soul and lacks compassion for the heart. While the Catholic clergyman in England is allowed to enter workhouses only with difficulty, if at all, in Ireland he is able to enter, although with certain restrictions. In Gorey a missioner was allowed to hold lectures, celebrate Mass and administer the Holy Sacraments for the Catholic inmates. I chose Father Van Antwerpen for this purpose because of his apostolic zeal and his extraordinary love for the poor. He went there every day. In the dining-room an altar was erected and he read the Holy Mass there. But according to the rules of the house, Protestant inmates were not allowed to attend the lectures or to participate in the Mass. At the end of the mission as we were eating dinner it happened that a twelve-year-old boy from this workhouse came in and demanded to be admitted into the Catholic Church. We asked him how it was possible for him to leave the workhouse in his uniform, as the exit was closely guarded and a constable would pick him up on the street. He told us that a tailor was in the workhouse on business, and when he left he went out with him, hiding to one side of the tailor so that the guard would not see him. Once outside, the darkness prevented the constable from recognising him. We asked him, furthermore, why he wanted to become a Catholic. He answered that he wanted to save his soul irrespective of the cost. We asked him further how he arrived at this idea. He told us then how he, as a Protestant, was not allowed to listen to the sermons of the Father. He nevertheless found a way to listen secretly to the sermons of the Father and thus learned that only the Catholic faith could make him happy.

We asked him if he did not know what would await him because he escaped and now wanted to become a Catholic. He answered yes, that he wanted to save his soul. After these answers we were all agreed that we had to help him, no matter what uncomfortable results our apostolic office would have to face. Father Van Antwerpen took over immediately and used the rest of the night to make a Catholic out of him. It turned out that he was more knowledgeable than we had anticipated. In short, on the next day in the church he was a complete Catholic. We also took care of his physical hunger and thirst. Then we advised him to return to the workhouse, because otherwise he would certainly be caught. He was fully determined to suffer for the sake of Jesus. When he arrived at the door, he was taken into custody and punished because he had secretly escaped. During his examination he revealed everything. He was told that he was not allowed to convert to Catholicism before he was fourteen years old. He answered: 'I am that already.' The following day the workhouse commission met and the new Catholic was brought before it. He requested that his name be expunged from the roster of Protestants and included in that of the Catholics. The commission answered: 'You are not allowed to convert before the age of fourteen.' He said: 'I am that already.' He had to request this inclusion in the register so that he could participate in the Catholic religious service. Our own mission in the workhouse was not impaired as a result of this occurrence, but the new Catholic was incarcerated, so that he could not listen to the Father's sermons. But he escaped by letting himself down from the window by using linen sheets from his bed, and thus he attended the sermon. He was consequently whipped so hard that he had to go to the workhouse hospital. There a Catholic woman said to him: 'They may mistreat your body but they cannot touch your soul.' These words he remembered well and repeated them often to himself, and thus took comfort in them. We felt it our duty to take care of him and we were able to get him out of the workhouse, whereupon he took Holy Communion and the Holy Sacrament of Confirmation.

Soon after this mission we conducted one in Wexford, a town of 12,000 Catholics plus a few Protestants. It is located twenty-one English miles south of Gorey on the sea and consequently has a harbour. It was here that Henry II landed when the English began the conquest of Ireland. This town had only one Catholic church, which belonged to the Franciscan Fathers, who had, however, come down very much in the world. But there was here also a parish priest who held services in the Franciscan church. But there were already two parish churches (*Pfarrkirchen*) under construction for which only the walls were standing. Further away on a hill overlooking the city there was a convent of the 'Sisters of Mercy' with a large chapel. In addition there was in the centre of the town another convent with a large chapel, belonging to the female Franciscans. Furthermore, below the 'Sisters of Mercy' cloister there was a church belonging to the bishop's diocesan seminary in which, however, there was very little space for the laity. Wexford belongs to the diocese of Ferns, which [place] is now no more than a village. Formerly it was a royal residence, whose king was at war with others in Ireland over a kidnapping. He called upon Henry II of England for help, who came but never left Ireland. The bishop resides in Enniscorthy, a town between Gorey and Wexford.

I went there first to observe everything and make arrangements. I arranged everything with the priest[41] as in Omagh and Gorey. A wealthy bachelor named Devereux turned his house over to me.[42] He told me that he would stay with his brother near the town. His house contained a nice chapel. He also offered to pay for our upkeep, but I refused that offer and gave him the following reasons: 'Firstly, we have to work hard, and therefore we eat and drink only what is necessary in order to keep up our energy. But we eat and drink only what is necessary, nothing superfluous or costly, avoiding any luxury and eating and drinking what is normal for the middle class. If we accepted your offer, you would, because of your love, treat us like upper-class "gentlemen", a position that would not well suit us as missioners to the poor. Therefore we must insist that we take care of our own meals. My second reason', I said, 'is as follows: we want to take care of our work as completely as possible, and that requires much time. We do not intend to stay here one day more than is necessary, but we will remain until our task is done. If you took care of our expenses, then we would be constantly afraid that we are taking advantage of your generosity, and we would try to hurry things to end the mission before our task was completed. If you wish to do something for the good work, you are free to do so, but your donations to me must be completely at my disposal for our needs.' I also rejected all invitations with the statement that it would be unseemly for us as preachers to the poor to be eating in the homes of the rich.

This, my speech, was publicised all over the city and made an excellent impression and generally increased the respect for us all. Several weeks later I arrived with six missioners, and therefore there were seven of us. And the seven of us worked here for six weeks. Father Douglas was the bursar. Father Furniss, with the help of Father Vanderstichele, was the missioner to the children. Devereux's two servants took care of us. We were so very well supported here that we made a profit on top of it all. During the last week here we gave only two or at most three sermons because we wanted to concentrate on hearing confessions. In this respect Father Van Antwerpen excelled with his popular catechism. He gave three sermons on the 7th Commandment, and in the introduction to the 3rd sermon he demonstrated how the common people transgressed against this commandment. But there were also rich distinguished people in that category, and he had to talk about them as well. At that point he gave a number of examples and spelled out exactly how precisely and substantively these cases differed in detail and how these obligations were ignored. I saw in that connection how important he was as confessor-priest. He was the simplest and humblest soul. Unfortunately this was his last mission. I saw towards the end of the mission that he required rest. I therefore sent him home, where shortly after his arrival he died of typhus. He was thirty-three years old. We received the message of his death while on the mission in Strabane. We wept over his death as that of a loving and valuable brother who always worked hard. This mission [Wexford] was the best and most brilliant that was held under my direction. That was twenty years ago, and it is still clearly in the people's memory, as a priest wrote to me in 1874. Also our Fathers who conducted a mission there last year wrote to me about the earlier mission.

Two boys from the workhouse in Gorey came to this mission. One of them was thereupon released. He received a certificate of his freedom and street clothes. The other one escaped secretly and had no papers and still wore the workhouse garb. They [the workhouse officials] probably realised that he would eventually be caught and returned. To prevent this the two boys exchanged their clothing with each other. The one who escaped with the street clothes of the other boy escaped detection. The one with the uniform of the workhouse also was not bothered because he had the right papers. Father Van Antwerpen took care of these poor fellows and found a good place for them.

During the mission I heard that Father Held, still vice-provincial for England, etc., was coming from London in order to observe what was going on. Since he was going to Limerick anyhow, I invited him to come to Wexford at the end of the mission. He came at exactly the right time. Father Coffin as prefect of the church arranged everything for the finale. This had to be held in the open air so that there would be no accident with the large crowd that was expected. For that purpose a large square in front of the church and surrounded by trees was used. It was also surrounded by houses from which everything could be seen and heard. It began to rain, and I asked Father Douglas to pray to the Child Jesus that we might end this mission with good weather. This humble and obedient man prayed, and thus we were able to conclude our mission in the open air. Father Held led the procession *cum Sanctissimo* [with the Blessed Sacrament] and gave the customary blessing. I gave the final sermon. The whole square and the neighbouring street was tightly packed with people. All the windows in the houses were filled with spectators, as well as the roofs, and the trees were full of boys as if they were gathering fruit and pears.

The overall impression that the mission made can be demonstrated by the following. The next day we left in three groups. Two or three of our Fathers went in the first carriage to go back to Liverpool. A crowd accompanied them for a half-hour. The others, except Father Held and myself, took the other carriage in the direction of Limerick and were accompanied for nearly an hour. Father Held and I wanted to visit the bishop[43] before we left. He lived in the neighbourhood. We returned home by twelve o'clock noon and ordered our dinner for one o'clock. As we sat there quietly we learned about the festive accompaniment of our Fathers on part of the people. I said to Father Held: 'We can easily leave because no one knows the time of our departure.' We had ordered the carriage for two o'clock. While we were thus quietly talking with each other, we noticed a great gathering of people in front of the house. I said to Father Held: 'We will leave by the back door and thus escape from the view of the crowd.' I went to order the gate in the back yard to be closed in order that no one could get in. But the yard was already full of people. An escape was impossible, and we had to accept our fate. At two o'clock our carriage arrived, and I saw a large number of carriages behind it in the street. I said to Father Held: 'Let us go', but our passage through the street was closed off by the crowd. We had trouble getting to the carriage. The goodbyes had no end. We had already said our goodbyes the night before to the parish clergyman and other clerics and Mr Devereux, etc. The priest insisted that we should eat dinner with him. Following my principles I declined, but promised that we would visit them in the evening for a cup of tea.

This was the evening of the end of our mission. The priest had already invited other gentlemen, but besides the tea the priest had provided many other things that cost him more than a dinner. I noticed this subterfuge and determined that in the future I would no longer accept such an invitation. Then we went back to our carriage, which could move forward only very slowly through the heavy crowd. All the stores in the streets through which we went were closed as if it were a high holiday. But all the windows were open, with ladies in them waving their handkerchiefs at us. At the edge of the town all the children of the large orphanage in Wexford were standing with their banner, which they presented us as a gift. The people accompanied us for an hour. I asked them with great emphasis to go back. Finally they allowed us to travel more quickly. We two brought our breviaries and read our office for half an hour. Then Father Held noticed a large number of carriages that were accompanying us. There were eighty carriages with the 'elite' of the town, including the mayor. The latter was formerly *quoad religionem valde notae* [in regard to religion strongly stigmatised]. He lived in a mixed marriage (*gemischten Ehe*), but the mission converted him. I jumped immediately from my carriage in order to prevent them from going further. At that point they all jumped from their carriages and surrounded me. I thanked them for their great love and appreciation and blessed them and told them to go home. Then the mayor kneeled down and wept like a humble servant. After repeated goodbyes we departed. Several youths accompanied us to the next church, where they entered and prayed for us. Father Held himself said that he had never seen anything like it.

## V. Cork

The purpose of our trip was to visit New Ross, where we made a preliminary 'arrangement' with the parish priest for our next mission. Then we travelled to Limerick via Waterford, where the rest of our group was waiting for us in a rented house at Bank Place. Father Held was there because of our expected establishment of a branch house. What happened there and what we agreed to, I have forgotten. I only remember going from there to Cork in order to make arrangements with the very worthy Bishop Delany[44] for the use of his cathedral for a mission. Cork was 3rd largest city according to population in Ireland, with a magnificent harbour. It is also the home town of the famous Lola Montez who is Irish and not Spanish. Formerly she was married to an English officer named Brown [*sic*]. She left him and took the name Lola Montez,[45] and travelled around as a dancer. She was probably a member of a secret society that needed female agents to advance its purpose. Catholic Munich, with its excellent university, was for a long time a thorn in the side of these secret societies. They were able to destroy Catholic Bavaria through its King Ludwig, and they used Lola Montez for this purpose. After the Munich burghers chased her out she went to Switzerland, where she was fêted by the Freemasons. She then went to London, where she bewitched a highly placed rich young 'gentleman' into marrying her. The entire family of the 'gentleman' was full of consternation about this. His name was Heald. His family discovered that she had been previously married to the officer Brown, who was still alive and who sued her. She then escaped to the US, where she collected money for the purpose of liberating Bavaria from the Jesuits. The Americans allowed themselves to be bewitched by her. From there she went to Australia, and she returned from there to Europe. After the young Mr Heald was freed from her grasp, the case against her was dropped. Then she gave lectures in London on how women can make themselves interesting and beloved by men. These lectures were published. I also got hold of them. Her language was decent. She supposedly died in poverty.

At that time there were four parish churches (*Pfarreien*) in Cork, a Capuchin convent, a Franciscan convent, a Dominican convent and two monasteries of Christian Brothers. These were teaching brothers of two types. Those of the first type were called Presentation Brothers; they conformed more in their schools to the English laws and consequently received support from the state. The other group took a more rigorous attitude and refused all support from the state and thereby retained their independence. The latter also received me into their house on my first visit. They formed with those in Limerick a national body. There was in Cork also a cloister of Presentation nuns who organised and staffed the female schools. Nearer the harbour there was an Ursuline convent at Blackrock. The community was the first that was established after the persecution ended. It was very numerous, and the educational institution was in all respects outstanding. I visited them at various times and preached there, and a close friendly relationship developed between them and me. The Vincentians also had a school here.

My meeting with the very worthy bishop was very warm. I talked with him about the plans for the mission. He lived outside of the city, near the Ursuline convent. But he also had a house within the city next to the cathedral, which was empty. He came to it two or three times a week and held audiences. This house was perfect for our purposes. I hoped that we would have as successful a mission here as we had in Wexford. But it turned out differently, as I will relate. Thereafter we held a mission in the north of Ireland in Strabane between Omagh and Londonderry, similar to the ones in Gorey and Wexford. Father Furniss worked in all these missions with great distinction. His mission to the children gave our mission its unique brilliance. How long we worked there I do not remember any more. The house in which we lived there [Strabane] was too small. A neighbouring Presbyterian offered us several rooms. God rewarded him for that with the grace of conversion for him and his entire family. Here it was that Father Douglas was called to Rome by the very worthy Father Smetana.[46] We were very unhappy at losing him. He was not a brilliant preacher, but was an excellent confessor and performed his duties as bursar humbly and to everyone's satisfaction. Where we went thereafter I do not remember.

During this period I also had to give a retreat for the priests of the entire diocese in the bishop's college in Wexford. There is a rule there that each priest is to make such a retreat every two years, one year the parish priests and the other year the curates. These retreats lasted one week. The bishop attended, as well as his vicar general and the professors of the college. I had at one time held a retreat in the Tyrol in Neustif near Brixen and was consequently prepared. But now I had to give them in English. But I was so exhausted by this time that my head was nailed up (*Kopf wie vernagelt*). And it remained nailed up until the beginning of the retreat. I could not clear my head and was consequently prepared for much embarrassment. This feeling of a nailed-up head continued during my trip there. My trip to Wexford was by way of Gorey, where we had had the beautiful mission. The priest there[47] invited me to stay overnight with him. We would then on the next day, a Sunday, travel together to Wexford. When I arrived there [Gorey], he asked me to say Mass in his stead on Sunday and to give a sermon to the people. I agreed and said the Holy Mass and then gave a sermon. But I was forced to leave the altar without giving the sermon because my head was still tightly nailed up, to the surprise of the priest and his congregation. In the sacristy I made my apologies, referring to my head. We ate our big breakfast and then took off for Wexford. The bishop received us kindly, as did the priest. But the nailed-up condition of my head continued. I had to accept the fact and said to myself: 'Lord if you want to humble me in this way, thy will be done.' I had a very restless night.

On Monday the retreat was to begin early in the morning. All the dignitaries and the bishop were assembled. I kneeled down in front of the altar and said the *Veni Creator Spiritus* with a plea to the Mother of God. All of a sudden all of my tightness was gone and my head was clear. I was able to speak normally, and everything proceeded well and smoothly. The retreat was blessed, but I must confess: Lord, it is all your doing. The devotional service of the Stations of the Cross was especially impressive. There were those who warned me to leave this devotion alone. It was looked upon as a devotional service for the poor people but not for educated and scholarly persons. But I refused to concede this to them. And it was especially this devotional service that made the greatest impression. I experienced the same thing later, of which I will give several examples below. I forgot to mention before that we often replaced a sermon on the martyrdom of Christ with the Stations of the Cross and that it always made a great impression on the people. Even in the Tyrol in every mission the Stations of the Cross were done at least once. At every retreat that I conducted I included the devotional service of the Stations of the Cross because it was immeasurably useful and full of blessings. At the end of the retreat the entire body came with the vicar general[48] at their head to thank me. On this occasion the vicar general asked to be permitted to ask some questions. Naturally I allowed this request. He said: 'Formerly we always had a Jesuit for our retreat. And these Jesuits quoted very often from St Ignatius their founder. We expected that you would do the same with your founder, because we are all great admirers of St Alphonsus. It is true you mentioned him from time to time, but not in the volume that we had expected.' I answered: 'Gentlemen, you will have to excuse me. Everything I said is from St Alphonsus. It would not have been very seemly if I constantly said: "St Alphonsus, St Alphonsus".' Thereupon these gentlemen said: 'We are now satisfied.' This vicar general allowed a mission to be conducted in his parish,[49] but I did not participate in it. Why I no longer know, and at the same time other details have escaped me. I have to omit the mention of other missions and retreats.

During our mission in Wexford Father Held was still vice-provincial in England, even though recently he had to reside in Belgium, and Father Buggenoms was the local superior of Clapham. Shortly thereafter what I reported earlier, namely that Father Hacklik, consultor at Clapham, requested a visitation. Father Paul Reyners, former master of novices in Belgium, was sent as visitor. This visitation ended with Father Held's departure from the Congregation [in England]. The position of provincial for England was taken from Father Held, and Father Paul Reyners took over and at the same time became rector of Clapham house. Father Paul Reyners was a sick and weak man, whereas England needed a strong and active person.

Soon thereafter the province was divided into a Belgian and a Dutch–English province. Father Swinkels,[50] the present Bishop of Surinam, became our provincial. Father Reyners, the rector of Clapham, became his coadjutor with another Dutchman whose name I have forgotten. We found it very curious that the provincial would reside in Holland and his coadjutor in England. Father Swinkels visited our house in Liverpool once. I can no longer recall the reasons for this visit. They must have been very unimportant. Father Bernard Hafkenscheid[51] came from America, where he had been provincial, to reside in England. He was to become the superior of the new house in Limerick and to conduct the missions in Ireland from there. First he came to Liverpool. I was to acquaint him with the situation in Ireland and present him to the bishops. Exactly at that time the mission in New Ross was to take place. This was the last mission that I was to direct in Ireland. I introduced him everywhere in Ireland and presented him to all the great missioners from Holland and Belgium as the recent occupier of the office of provincial in America. We travelled together to the mission in New Ross, which was done in the same way in which we had done the others. Out of respect for Father Bernard (that is how he wanted to be called) I did not wish to appear as superior and left the honour to him and told my people to accept his benediction, which I also did. I did not receive from him, however, a reciprocal respect.

The mission went very well. I do not recall whether it took three or four weeks. The town of New Ross was somewhat smaller than Wexford and was not on the ocean. The harbour closest to New Ross was Waterford, which was three or four hours away, but steamships travelled between New Ross and Waterford. There was much work to be done, and the parish priest and the community wished the mission to last as long as that at Wexford. I mention this here as evidence that the missions will not prove to be exhausting when they are conducted according to the rules of St Alphonsus, whether they last fourteen days, or eight to ten days as our Fathers in Bavaria and Austria believe. To be sure, we could have conducted the mission as it is done in Austria and Bavaria, where it is more like an agitated hunt (*Hetzjagd*) and where there is little in the way of instruction and passions are constantly excited, whereas our missions were of longer duration, for otherwise we could not have [properly] sustained them. When the missions are held according to the rules of St Alphonsus, matters are different. We did not shy away from any work. Even though the mission in New Ross had lasted nearly four weeks, the enthusiasm was still great and the parish priest and the community asked us to remain there as long as we had in Wexford. Since our upkeep was met by voluntary gifts and no official accounting was necessary, no one felt burdened by the expenses. But Father Bernard used the authority that I had transferred to him to end the mission, to my displeasure and that of the parish priest and the community.

Father Bernard did not preach a sermon at this mission and excused himself before a deputation of the community because he did not speak English well. They answered him that they had observed exactly the opposite in their discussion with him. He allowed me to preach all the main sermons. I noticed at the same time that this was a sort of test for me. I tried hard not to show any lack of respect towards him. All the Fathers supported him since they were all Belgians and Hollanders, and also the English Fathers, who received their training in the Congregation in Belgium and Holland. I too honoured Father Bernard as a person with a great reputation as a missioner and as a scion of a rich family and as the recipient of a Roman doctorate, who had sacrificed everything for the Congregation. He had a well-deserved reputation as a missioner. I could not compare myself with him and felt inferior to him in every respect. In addition, I was an Austrian and was considered a follower of Father Smetana, which, however, was not the case. I knew Father Smetana's good qualities and accomplishments and honoured him for them. One certainly had to recognise that he brought order to the governance of the Congregation in that Father Passerat[52] [had] represented a more patriarchal administration. What one could criticise in him was his Austrian bureaucratic and absolutistic attitude. What one had to admire above all with Father Smetana was his broad scholarship in jurisprudence and theology. What he wrote was excellent. He wrote everything himself because no secretary could satisfy him. His first French letter was errorless; he was able to read English as well and had a total command of Latin. He was graduated *doctor utriusque juris* [doctor in civil and canon law]. He had turned over his estates in Moravia to his brother and became a simple Redemptorist.

The fight over poverty had broken out already between Smetana and the Belgians etc. Father Smetana was supported by the German and Austrian Fathers. They viewed the Belgians etc. as opponents of Father Passerat, who was extraordinarily respected in Belgium and Holland. I never completely understood the quarrel. Moreover, I had no time for such things, which seemed to me like chasing after a horse. Consequently I was never interested in talking about it. But my silence and my deep respect for the vicar general made it appear that I was in Smetana's camp. The justice of the Belgians' case against the Bavarians and Austrians was heightened by the financial speculations of the latter two, which the Belgians unanimously condemned. Moreover, they thought that the Austrians were too willing to submit to the government. Father Smetana viewed me as a supporter of his party. In addition, the Belgians saw many of my own failings and said so. My subordinates were all strict observers and viewed me as lax. And in part they were right. They had just come out of the novitiate and studies and were models of order, whereas I had travelled around much of the world outside of the Congregation *ex obedientia* [from obedience]. I consequently had lost my interest in details. I always had demonstrated my dedication, love and industriousness, to which I can testify before God *non quaesivi quae mea sunt sed quae congregationis* [I have not sought my own interests but only those of the Congregation]. But those who worked under me outdid me by far in punctuality and precision in the small details. But in the worldly (*zeitlich*) needs they never lacked anything; and I was always generous. I always inquired about their well-being, which was also held against me. They did not like my conferences either. I had little time to prepare myself for them. I chose something or other for them to read instead of working something out myself. I thought that that would be better for them. Besides, I am an enemy of everything rigorous because I was injured by that greatly during my youth. I have emphasised more brotherly love and forgiveness.

Moreover, during the entire period that I spent in England I was physically ill and suffered from constipation and vomiting. I was never capable of making a ten-day retreat.[53] The food and drink were all different from what I was used to. I sometimes had to have a special diet, which could be easily be misinterpreted. Young people tend easily to be censorious. Unfortunately I had the same fault in my own youth. I will give an example. In my youth I viewed the inability of old priests, who were unable to bend the knee fully during the Holy Mass, as terrible, but now I also cannot do it. How severely did I criticise the old priest Raymund in Mautern, and now I am in the same position. It remains true: having sinned in the past, one is now punished by the same means.

Where I went after the mission in New Ross I no longer remember. I do remember that the priest and some other gentlemen accompanied me a certain distance. We passed a lordly castle that belonged to the New Ross district. The priest told me that the owner had neither hands nor feet.[54] He was born with only stumps. His parents were formerly Catholic and left the church to become Protestants. On the day of his father's conversion the Protestant minister told him: 'Yesterday you were big people, but now you are small ones.' He was insulted by these words and asked for a clarification. The answer was that 'Yesterday you were a big man among the Catholics, but today you are only a small man among the Protestants.' This apostate nobleman wanted to prove himself a good Protestant and severed the hands and feet of a statue of the Mother of God in his castle. Thereupon his son was born without hands or feet. The priest added that his crippled landlord was an educated and decent person. He uses artificial hands, with which he is able to sign his name, and artificial feet so that he can travel.

I had to turn over all the missions that had been scheduled to Father Bernard and consequently also the one in the cathedral at Cork. I was asked to participate, however, which I did with pleasure along with two or three of my subordinates, Father Bernard knew how to make a mission exceptional. He also preached here and received much applause. The enthusiasm on this mission was huge. The people did not want to leave the confessional at night. They remained there all night so that they would not lose their place. It was impossible to shut the church, and it was lit the whole night through. All the priests had to hear confessions, and because there were not enough confessionals, old railroad carriages on the far side of the church square were used. A beautiful cross with a large figure of Christ was erected. It came from the estate of the great Daniel O'Connell, and it was a gift for this purpose. Father Bernard was able to make its consecration into a great festival. The same happened with the festival for the Mother of God. The Irish liked all this immensely. They love such externalities (*Ausserlichkeiten*). We too in our missions used festivals (*Feyerlichkeiten*) because they are very helpful, but Father Bernard had a special talent in that way. Moreover, in the cathedral in Cork there were more resources available. The very worthy bishop and the clergy were most co-operative. In addition to the festivities that he organised in accordance with our programme, he also was a spellbinding speaker. He knew how to kindle the passions of the Irish immensely.

The Irish are a sentimental people (*Gefuhlsmenschen*), and he who wishes to make himself beloved by them must appeal to their emotions. I praised their forebears, but I would not flatter them to their faces. I wanted them to see their errors, because today's Irish are not what their forebears were. With the end of the persecution their enthusiasm has greatly decreased. The complaint in England that the Irish make *sola fides* [only an interior commitment to faith] is not without foundation. Moreover a part — a goodly part — of the high and low clergy are willing to entertain a *modus vivendi* [manner of living] which the Primate, Dr Cullen, had to neutralise. I found among the bishops and priests no longer a simple faith but a critical attitude about Catholic belief. I realised also that foreign priests were necessary to reform the Irish clergy. Everywhere I saw the words of Christ proved: 'He who elevates himself, will be cast down.' This is especially true of the Irish, who consider themselves the best Catholics in the world and look down on all others. In a mission one cannot ignore sentiment, but reason must dominate. Our efforts were in that direction. And with the Irish this is necessary because with them enthusiasm from feeling clouds and diminishes introspection. Enthusiasm through feeling gives to a mission great external brilliance. That was Father Bernard's goal. That was, however, far from what I wanted to accomplish while I was in charge. We tried to use reason in order to develop the right feeling, which I think is the correct way of doing things. Father Bernard had good intentions. He wanted to make the missions credible, but I think that such credibility is transitory. The best credibility is solid work, and that is permanent. I mention this here deliberately because here in Austria the same mistake is being made in that the missioners look too much for external brilliance. It is the reason that the missions, here at least, have lost credibility. Less brilliance and more solidity, and their credibility will be restored.

It was always my basic principle when I worked as subordinate at a mission that I would not try to influence my superior. I followed this principle completely in my relationship with Father Bernard, and thus I allowed the following contradiction to occur, namely that Bernard sanctioned the bishops and clergy taking care of all our meals and the expenses of the mission. Thus he destroyed what we had constructed with such care. In that way the old evils that we had tried so hard to eliminate arose again. Thus the missions became more profitable. But that that was not the intention of St Alphonsus is clear. That missions should incur debts was also not to his purpose, nor to ours. By taking the expenditures into our own hands, we did not lose and might even have gained. It was a cause for general surprise that we wanted to control our own expenditures and that we would only take alms for that purpose. In time these alms would have flowed more copiously if we would have continued in this way and publicised the fact even more. But what I introduced in the Congregation, except for Italy, was a novelty. My unworthiness was of no importance. I had told Father Held my sentiments about this, and he had allowed me to do as I wished. Possibly Father Bernard and Father Reyners had not even bothered to investigate my reasons. Furthermore, Father Bernard needed money for the construction of the house in Limerick and Father Reyners was responsible for the upkeep of the houses in London and Liverpool. I may also have failed in that I remained silent when these changes were made. I remained silent because I thought that my views would be ignored and, moreover, because I did not want to start a fight. And in spite of the fact that I wanted to avoid a fight with Father Reyners and Father Bernard, I did get involved in one — and how! As soon as I got control over the expenditures of the missions, Father Held allowed me, at my request, to assign the Fathers to the saying of the Holy Mass.[55] I said if the Fathers were to take up quarters in another house, then they were to say Mass for its intentions, that is, as payment for their upkeep. When the Fathers came to me from Clapham, I not only took care of their upkeep but reimbursed them for their travel expenses as well, etc. *ergo* —. After Father Bernard overthrew my system and had the bishop or priest pay for the travel and take care of the meals and upkeep, my Fathers from Liverpool asked me if they also had to say Mass at the mission in Cork according to Father Bernard's interpretation. I answered: 'You say Mass according for the intention of the house in Bishop Eton until Father Bernard countermands the order.' Soon after the beginning of the mission in Cork Father Reyners also arrived. They placed me on the carpet and accused me of having forbidden my Fathers from Bishop Eton to say Mass according to the orders of 'their Superior'. This made me very angry. This was heightened by the fact that Father Bernard had written to my minister at Bishop Eton to send another Father. I accused him of having gone over my head as superior of that house. In my anger I said: 'Is this the reward for having allowed myself as an obedient servant to be degraded?' etc. etc. Father Reyners ordered me thereupon to beg Father Bernard's forgiveness, which I did. Thus the quarrel was smoothed over, but it remained heavy in my heart. How long the mission lasted in Cork I do not remember. But it was clear that he did not want to extend the mission in Cork, as he had already demonstrated in New Ross.

I held another mission with Father Bernard in the parish of the vicar general on the southside of Cork, but I do not remember when. Father Furniss served in both missions as missioner to the children. In the General Chapter he [Bernard] showed later his displeasure with the mission to the children as a mission within a mission. If I had been there, I would have told him: 'That is as St Alphonsus wanted it.' In both of the missions in Cork we had a highly unpleasant occurrence take place in the church. In the mission in the cathedral church the instruction to the women was conducted behind closed doors. After it was over the people stormed the doors. In order for the women to be able to leave, we opened one door. At the same time the people pushed in at the other door, and then the women became hysterical and caused a blockage of their exit. The priests tried to pry them loose but were unable to do so. This lasted until we were able to get the women in the rear to be reasonable and to back off, but this brought about such confusion that one woman broke her foot.

At the 2nd mission I preached the evening sermon. Afterwards I went into the sacristy to hear confessions and the parish priest gave the Benediction. All of a sudden the people ran through the sacristy yelling 'Fire!' Therefore I ran into the church to see what was wrong. The priest was still in the pulpit attempting to restore order, but there was so much noise that one could not hear one's own words. Everyone rushed out of the church. I tried to yell as loudly as possible, but I could not even hear myself. Then I made a sign to the organist that he should start to play, and I myself kneeled down in order to pray. This helped to restore order in the church. I then went into the sacristy, and Father Bernard came and said: 'Quick, quick! Help the dying!' At that point a woman was brought into the sacristy who was bent over with pain. Outside at the wall there were several persons who had fainted. Several others were brought to the hospital. What had happened? It appeared that some [building material] had fallen from the scaffolding, and one person thought the whole scaffold was collapsing. This caused all the confusion. The platform was as secure as ever. Luckily no one broke any bones. There were only a few people who fainted or were bruised.

No one died, and everyone recovered quickly. The sight of all this chaos could be upsetting, and someone who has never seen this cannot appreciate it. It was probably the work of some rascals. A young rascal tried the same thing in a children's mission in Liverpool in St Patrick's. On the following day we explained to the people and cautioned them not to excite themselves when they heard such a cry. With the problem at the door of the cathedral with the women, I understood also the great accident that happened in the cathedral in San Lago in Chili [*sic*].

I have already said that what some saw as luxury under my direction resulted in missions that were much more disciplined than those that came later. I was forbidden to put wine on the table. I obeyed. But later the wine appeared again. We accepted no invitations during a mission, but that was changed in the end. I have already said how our missions won credibility when we took care of our upkeep. Our unselfishness and sacrifice was admired. We were also praised for adhering to St Alphonsus's rule to continue the mission until it had achieved its objective. When Father Bernard changed this, the Redemptorists lost credibility. When Father Bernard began building our house in Limerick, he sent Father Petcherine to Wexford to Mr Devereux, in whose house we lived during the mission there, and who was generous in everything. He contributed to every undertaking. He liked Father Petcherine very much. Following Petcherine's request, Devereux gave the following answer: 'You have no money for your missions, and consequently I will not give you any for your house.' Father Petcherine told me this himself.

I do not recall where we went after the 2nd mission in Cork. But I do recall preaching to the 'Sisters of Mercy' in Cork while their house was being constructed and also to the Ursulines. I felt especially comfortable with the Ursulines. They allowed me to participate in their recreation (*Rekreation*), which they did with the bishop's permission. They showed me there a large piece of the [True] Cross, the size of a forefinger. This part of the Cross came to Ireland before the Reformation with the requirement that a Cistercian monastery be erected. At the time of Henry VIII it was almost finished. Because of the persecution that followed, it could not be completed. I myself saw the ruins.

The part of the Cross was secured by giving it to a pious family under the condition that it be given over to the first monastery that was built after the persecutions ceased. This first convent was that of the Ursulines in Cork, and they thus received the relic. Because its authentication was lost, it could not be venerated. I thought it was authentic enough for me, and I begged to have a piece of it. But it was denied me because the bishop had ordered that it stay intact. Father Bernard invited me to Limerick in order to preach during All Souls' week. When I arrived there, I was completely astounded by his entrepreneurial spirit. He had already acquired a plot of land that we had wanted but could not get. A City Hall and a temporary church, which was fairly large, already stood on it. Windows, doors and benches could be used for the new building. We Austrians are far behind in the speed and the cleverness with which this was done. Later[56] Father Bernard conducted a mission in the west of Ireland in Galway.During this period I conducted a retreat for the clergy in Tuam somewhat to the north of Galway, whose archbishop was MacHale, who was called the Lion of Ireland.[57] He was very active in Catholic journalism. The energy with which he spoke created astonishment. He was also the first who signed himself everywhere as Archbishop of Tuam in spite of the Ecclesiastical Titles Bill.[58] This time all the priests of the diocese were again invited to participate in the retreat. I was a little worried about this man. But how surprised I was when I entered his house. A nice, old, humble priest received me. We sat there together in brotherly fashion. Next to his house he had a sort of *collegium*, whose pupils were on holiday during the retreat. The priests were lodged in this building. The retreat lasted one week. The archbishop was also able to read German as well as being a Greek scholar. Opposite his house was a park and the palace of the Protestant Bishop of Tuam, but the cathedral church of this Protestant bishop, with a pitiful tower, was no larger than the poorest village church in Austria. He has so few parishioners in Tuam that they do not fill up even a ¼ part of this little church. In opposition there stood the stately Catholic cathedral church in a most awe-inspiring location. It was a creation of the present archbishop. English was spoken only in the little town of Tuam. All the country folk spoke Irish. The cathedral was reserved for the retreat, except when Mass was being said. The high altar came from Rome and was a facsimile of that at St Caecilia's in Rome. As usual at such retreats, the Stations of the Cross were also conducted. The Stations of the Cross were in the church, but the devotion there was not much practised. To begin with I preached the Way of the Cross, according to St Alphonsus, whereupon the archbishop said: 'This devotional service is beautiful.' And I answered: 'Yes, it would be even more beautiful if it were celebrated in a festive manner.' He said: 'How so?' So I told him he should authorise me to choose the most honourable priests to carry the cross accompanied by two candle-bearers, and that all the priests would follow in procession. Then I wanted to have a priest with a good voice to pray out loud and with clearness. The archbishop must conclude the procession in mochetta and mozzetta with two assistants. Then we should sing a verse of the *Stabat Mater* between each station. Furthermore, we should let the people participate in this devotion.

The archbishop liked this and ordered that it should be done on the following day. The archbishop was delighted, and the people looked on with great wonderment. The archbishop translated the *Stabat Mater* into Irish that night and had copies made of it so that it could be sung in Irish.[59] This caused such devotion and such enthusiasm that the entire church was filled for this service. It made an even bigger impression with the priests. That was my last work in Ireland. I preached also twice before the people in the cathedral of Tuam and held several conferences for the nuns.

## Notes to Introduction

1 S. J. Boland, *A Dictionary of the Redemptorists* (Rome, 1987), pp. 303–4.
2 Joseph Prost, 'My Experiences from the Time of My Return from America in 1843 to the Present 1874', Notebook III, p. 114: Archives of the Austrian Redemptorist Province, Vienna.
3 Ibid., p. 124.
4 Edward Hosp, 'First Redemptorist Mission in Ireland', *Spicilegium Historicum Congregationis Sanctissimi Redemptoris*, viii, 2 (1960), p. 453.
5 Joseph Prost, 'Founding the Redemptorist Congregation in the USA, 1832–1843', *Social Justice Review*, transl. by Raymond J. Miller, C.Ss.R. (Sept. 1971), p. 168.
6 Ibid. Oct. 1971–Mar. 1973, *passim*.
7 Ibid. Apr. 1973, p. 31.
8 Ibid. p. 32.
9 John Sharp, *Reapers of the Harvest: The Redemptorists in Great Britain and Ireland, 1843–1898* (Dublin, 1989), p. 14.
10 Prost, 'My Experiences, 1843–1874', Notebook II, p. l.
11 S. J. Boland, 'Early Redemptorist Missions in England and Ireland (1848–1865)', *Spicilegium Historicum Congregationis Sanctissimi Redemptoris*, xxxiii, 2 (1985), p. 293.
12 Ibid.
13 See tabulated itinerary, pp. 16–17.
14 Michael Baily, 'The Mission Method of the First Superior of Missions in Ireland, Fr Joseph Prost (1804–1885)', Search, iii, 3 (spring 1987), pp. 11–13.
15 Prost, 'Founding the Redemptorist Congregation in the USA (June 1971), p. 98.
16 Joseph Prost, 'My Experiences in England, Ireland and the West Indies', Notebook V, p. 43: Archives of Austrian Redemptorist Province, Vienna.
17 Ibid.
18 John Guaci, 'The Mission of the Antilles', *Redemptorist North American Historical Bulletin*, 26 Apr. 1996, pp. 3–4.
19 Ibid. p. 5
20 Prost, 'My Experiences in England, Ireland and the West Indies', Notebook V, p. 83.
21 Prost, 'My Experiences, 1843–74,' Notebook IV, p. 2.
22 Ibid.
23 Alfred Schedl, 'Das Ringen um Eine Zeitgerechte Volksmission in Oesterreich', *Spicilegium Historicum Congregationis Sanctissimi Redemptoris*, xxxiii, 1 (1985), p. 234.
24 Prost, 'My Experiences, 1843–1874', Notebook IV, pp. 11–12.

25 Ibid. p. 14.

26 Ibid. p. 197.

27 Boland, *Dictionary*, p. 504.

28 Emmet Larkin, 'The Parish Mission Movement in Ireland, 1850–1880' (unpublished paper), p. 1.

29 Ibid.

30 Sharp, *Reapers of the Harvest*, p. 148.

31 *Manual of the Archconfraternity of the Holy Family* (Limerick, 1888), p. 4. Redemptorist Archives, Mount St Alphonsus, Limerick.

32 These figures are taken from the various *Elenchi*, or summary tables, that were compiled from the annals of each year's 'Apostolic Labours'. See tables for 1881–1900: Redemptorist Archives, Mount St Alphonsus, Limerick.

33 Ibid. 1901–10.

34 Larkin, 'Parish Mission Movement', pp. 5–6.

## Notes to Narrative

1 St Alphonsus de Liguouri (1696–1787), Italian churchman, Doctor of the Church, founder of the Congregation of the Most Holy Redeemer in Naples in 1732. His teaching in moral theology, equi-probabilism, has become standard in the Roman Catholic Church.

2 John Milner, Vicar Apostolic of the Western District of England (1803–26).

3 Catherine McAuley (1787–1841), founder of the Sisters of Mercy in Dublin in 1831.

4 Daniel Murray, Archbishop of Dublin (1823–52).

5 Paul Cullen, Archbishop of Armagh (1849–52), and Archbishop of Dublin (1852–78).

6 Theobald Mathew, O.F.M.Cap. (1790–1856), leader of temperance movement in Ireland (1838–46).

7 John Ryan, Bishop of Limerick (1828–64).

8 There have been traditionally two Roman Catholic Primates in Ireland. The Archbishop of Armagh is the Primate of All Ireland, while the Archbishop of Dublin is the Primate of Ireland.

9 Cornelius Denvir, Bishop of Down and Connor (1835–65).

10 The number of Protestants in Limerick in 1851 was about 5,000.

11 Madame Emille de Baligand, mother superior of the Good Shepherd Convent in Limerick.

12 Mr Sharples was most likely a relative of James Sharples, Bishop of Samaria, coadjutor to the Vicar Apostolic of the Lancashire District (1843–50).

13 William Monsell (1812–94), MP for County Limerick (1847–74), Baron Emly (1874). Monsell converted to Catholicism in 1850.

14 Henry William Wilberforce (1807–73), fourth son of William Wilberforce.

15 William Wilberforce (1759–33), MP for Yorkshire (1784–1812).

16 Samuel Wilberforce (1805–73), third son of William Wilberforce.

17 Robert Isaac Wilberforce (1802–57), second son of William Wilberforce.

18 John Bergin, Franciscan Guardian, Limerick.

19 Nicholas Patrick Stephen Wiseman, Cardinal Archbishop of Westminster (1850–65).

20 Sir Edward Richard Wyndham (1812–71), third Earl of Dunraven and first Baron Kenry of the United Kingdom

21 Louis de Buggenoms, C.Ss.R. (1816–82), superior, Limerick (1853–54).

22 Frederick de Held, C.Ss.R. (1779–81), provincial of Belgian province (1841–47), Vistor of England (1848–54).

23 This riot most likely took place in the summer of 1853.

24 William Higgin, Church of Ireland Bishop of Limerick (1849–53).

25 William Henry Hall, Mayor of Limerick (1853)

26 Daniel William Cahill, D.D. (1796–1864), popular Catholic lecturer, and sometime Professor of Natural Philosphy at Carlow College. He lectured on natural science in Ireland, the United States and Canada.

27 Prost substituted for Cahill about 6 July 1853 at St Michael's Church in Limerick for the benefit of the Mount St Vincent female orphanage in Limerick conducted by the Sisters of Mercy.

28 John Baptist Lans, C.Ss.R. (1808–86), superior, Bishop Eton (1854).

29 Prost's memory apparently failed him here. The general election of June–July 1852 did result in some anti-Catholic rioting, especially at Stockport in England, but there were no disturbances in Enniskillen. What most likely took place was that Prost felt that the Redemptorists holding a mission in Enniskillen so soon after the general election would be taken by the Orangemen of that town as a provocation, and it was more prudent, therefore, to postpone it. Indeed, the mission did not take place until 12 September 1852.

30 Daniel Boylan, Dean of Clogher, P.P. Enniskillen.

31 Charles MacNally, Bishop of Clogher (1843–64).

32 Thomas Meehan.

33 In fact the diocesan dignitary present on this occasion was not the Bishop of Derry (John MacLaughlin) but his coadjutor, Francis Kelly (1849–64).

34 Patrick MacGettigan, Bishop of Raphoe (1820–61).

35 Prost's memory of the sequence of events is not correct. He is apparently confusing Letterkenny, which he visited before Christmas 1852, with Omagh, where he opened the mission on 3 January 1853.

36 Daniel MacGettigan, C.C. Conwall and Leek, diocese of Raphoe, and coadjutor to the Bishop of Raphoe (1856–70).

37 The term *patrimonium* refers to the property inherited by a Redemptorist, which he could hold in his own name, but the use of which and the income from which was highly regulated and restricted by the Congregation.

38 Henry Harbison, C.Ss.R. (1820–88), entered the Redemptorist novitiate in 1853.

39 There were ten gulden to the pound, and two to the dollar about 1850.

40 A taler was worth two-and-a-half gulden.

41 James Roche, P.P. Wexford, diocese of Ferns.

42 Richard Devereux, of Wexford, was a generous benafactor of Catholic institutions and causes.

43 Myles Murphy, Bishop of Ferns (1850–56).

44 William Delany, Bishop of Cork (1847–86).

45 Lola Montez (1818–61) was born Marie Dolores Eliza Rosanna Gilbert in Limerick. She married her first husband, Captain Thomas James, in 1837. He sued for divorce in 1842. Gilbert began her career as a dancer and assumed the stage name of Lola Montez and a Spanish identity in the following year. Her liaison with the King of Bavaria, Ludwig Carl Augustus, began in 1847, and she exercised considerable influence over the government until Ludwig was forced to abdicate in March 1848. Montez returned to England and married George Trafford Heald in July 1849. Heald's guardian charged her with bigamy because her divorce of 1842 had not been finalised. After leaving the stage, Montez pursued a successful career as a public lecturer. She died in 1861 in New York.

46 Rudolph von Smetana, C.Ss.R. (1802–71), Vicar General of Transalpine Congregation (1850–55).

47 John Lacy, P.P. Gorey, diocese of Ferns.

48 Patrick Murphy, P.P., V.G., Glynn, diocese of Ferns.

49 The Redemptorists held a mission in Glynn and Barntown from 5 July to 28 July 1854.

50 Johan Baptist Swinkels, C.Ss.R. (1810–75), provincial of Anglo-Dutch province (1855–65).

51 Bernard Hafkenscheid, C.Ss.R. (1807–65), provincial of American province (1850–53), superior, Limerick (1854–55).

52 Joseph Passerat, C.Ss.R. (1772–1868), Vicar General of Transalpine Congregation (1820–48).

53 Redemptorist requirement once a year.

54 Arthur MacMorrough Kavanagh (1831–89) was a well-known sportsman and politician; MP for Co. Wexford (1866–68) and for Co. Carlow (1868–80). He succeeded to the family estates of some 29,000 acres in 1854, of which some 5,000 acres were located near New Ross in Co. Wexford.

55 The occasion for the quarrel between Prost and Hafkenscheid was over the question of mass intentions and the disposition of the stipends associated with them. A Catholic who wanted a mass said for the benefit of his own soul, or for that of another, made an offering to the priest for the saying of the mass. The superior of the house assigned the saying of those masses to the priests of the community, who were allowed to say one mass on weekdays, two on Sundays and festivals, and three on Christmas Day, and used the offerings or stipends for the support of the community. As superior of the parish missions, Prost obliged the fathers who served on the parish missions to say mass for the support of the missions. When Hafkenscheid succeeded Prost as superior of the parish missions and obliged the bishops and parish priests to bear the expenses of the missions, he also required the fathers on the missions to say mass according to the intention of the house in Limerick of which he was also the superior. When the fathers of Bishop Eton then asked Prost, who was their immediate superior, according to whose intention they were to say mass, Prost replied that it was to be for the intention of their own house; eventually Hafkenscheid directly countermanded this order — hence the quarrel.

56 This should be earlier rather than 'later', since the mission opened in Athenry on 29 September 1854.

57 John MacHale, Archbishop of Tuam (1834–81), popularly known as 'the Lion of St Jarlath's' or 'the Lion of the Tribe of Judah'.

58 Under the Ecclesiastical Titles Act of August 1851 (14 & 15 Vict., c. 60), the papal assignation of territorial titles to the Roman Catholic hierarchy in Ireland and Britain was declared unlawful and void.

59 This translation was later published by MacHale as *Topar na Croice* (Dublin, 1855).

## Bibliography

Baily, Michael, 'The Mission Method of the First Superior of Missions in Ireland, Fr Joseph Prost (1804–1885)', *Search*, iii, 3 (spring 1987), pp. 11–13

Boland, S. J., 'Early Redemptorist Missions in England and Ireland (1848–1865)', *Spicilegium Historicum Congregationis Sanctissimi Redemptoris*, xxxiii, 2 (1985), pp. 283–320

—— *A Dictionary of the Redemptorists* (Rome, 1987)

Claessens, P., *The Life of Father Bernard, C.Ss.R.: The Apostolate of a Redemptorist* (London, 1875)

Curley, Michael J., 'The Redemptorist Pioneers in America, 1832–1839', *Spicilegium Historicum Congregationis Sanctissimi Redemptoris*, iv (1956), pp. 121–55

Day, Edward, 'The Beginnings of the Redemptorists in the United States: 1832–1840' (Licentiate thesis, Catholic University of Louvain, 1958)

Dilkskron, F. P., *Rudolf von Smetana: Ein Beitrag zur Geschicte der Kongregation des Allerheiligsten Erlösers* (Vienna, 1902)

Gauci, John, 'The Mission of the Antilles', *Redemptorist North American Historical Bulletin*, 26 Apr. 1996, pp. 3–6

Girouille, Henri, *Vie du Vénérable Père Joseph Passerat, Premier Rédemptoriste Français, 1772–1858* (Paris, 1924)

Hosp, Edward, 'First Redemptorist Mission in Ireland', *Spicilegium Historicum Congregationis Sanctissimi Redemptoris*, viii, 2 (1960), pp. 453–85

Knab, Raymund, 'Father Joseph Prost, Pioneer Redemptorist in the United States', *Historical Records and Studies*, xxii (1932), pp. 32–84

Larkin, Emmet, 'The Devotional Revolution in Ireland, 1850–1875', *American Historical Review*, lxxvii (1972), pp. 625–52

—— *The Making of the Roman Catholic Church in Ireland, 1850–1860* (Chapel Hill, 1980)

—— 'The Parish Mission Movement in Ireland, 1850–1880' (unpublished paper)

Liguori, St Alphonsus de, *Complete Works*, xv: *Preaching*, ed. and transl. Eugene Grimm (New York, 1890)

Livius, Thomas, 'Father Furniss and his Work for Children' (London, 1896)

Meulemeester, Maurice de, *Le Père Frédéric von Held, Redemptoriste* (Jette, 1911)

O'Donnell, Patrick, 'Foundation of Limerick', *Search*, ii (1978), pp. 9–18

Prost, Joseph, 'Founding the Redemptorist Mission in the USA, 1832–1843', *Social Justice Review*, June 1971 – May 1973, transl. Raymond J. Miller

Schedl, Alfred, 'Das Ringen um Eine Zeitgerechte Volksmission in Oesterreich', *Spicilegium Historicum Congregationis Sanctissimi Redemptoris*, xxxiii, 1 (1985), pp. 229–41

Shepherd, C. 'A Forgotten Apostle: John Furniss,C. Ss. R. (1809–65)', *Clergy Review*, lxiii (1978), pp. 99–104

# Index